MW00713401

The Angel's Healing Love: Abundant Blessings from Above

The Angel's Healing Love: Abundant Blessings from Above

1st Edition

Copyright © Laura L. Smith 2012. All rights reserved. To contact the author: photographybylaura@earthlink.net.

Cover artwork "Angel with Heart" © 1999 Laura L. Smith.
Back cover cat photo "Dreaming of You" © 2012
Cat photos in book © 2012 Laura L. Smith
Author photo taken by Laura L. Smith.
Cat photos information: www.photographyplusbylaura.com

ISBN-13:9780615728322

Dedicated to all the LOVING souls I have known, alive and passed on. And to my wonderful children, Elizabeth and David, and grandchildren who have been with me through a zillion lifetimes.

Contents

The Angel's Healing Love: Abundant Blessings from Above

Introduction

Hello there blessed soul. Are you ready to accept the truth and change your life? **GOD**, the universe and your **ANGELS** have brought you to this book. These writings are meant for those who are **SPIRITUALLY** ready to learn and understand in order to advance in their **SPIRITUAL** journey. You will know because I am casting my pearls of wisdom out for all to take. And depending upon the reader's level of **SPIRITUAL** development and understanding, the pearls will be either transformed into a necklace, bracelet or ring.

SPIRITUAL growth means several things. It is being happy in the present regardless of what our past was. It is letting go of a self centered ego that keeps us in a negative state of being. It means understanding our part in the current life time and taking responsibility for our choices and not blaming others. It is the willingness to share **LOVE** with others and be thankful for what **GOD**, the universe and our **ANGELS** have bestowed upon us. It is the wisdom of life and the respect and **LOVE** of us and others.

Over the years I have noted that many people have no idea what their life purpose is in this current lifetime. They also do not understand how the universal energy works and how it interplays in their lives. As a result they blunder through life blinded by ego and make the same mistakes over and over again. They are not happy with their lives, they gossip and complain, are over sensitive to mundane things said to them and react negatively to minor issues they encounter. Then they wonder why they have so many problems in their life. At the end of their lives, these people pass on to the other side without achieving their earthly mission.

Learning about how to achieve **HAPPINESS** and balance in one's life requires letting go of a selfish centered ego and the programmed negative thought patterns that rules ones current lifestyle. It is a challenging life changing event that will change a person into a confident, **PEACEFUL** and **LOVING** person. Because of the change, the person's friends and or their significant other may feel threatened by the changes and ends their relationship with the person. The person's parents and siblings may not be supportive of the person's new outlook on life and dismiss it as rhetoric. The person may change occupations, and may give away possessions they feel they no longer need. Or the person will find themselves sharing more of what they have with others.

The above statements may cause the reader to feel anxiety, fear or anger. Those emotions are due to our ego and programming reacting to the very idea of loss. If a person is not ready to accept **HAPPINESS** and balance by letting go of self centered ego and the negative programming; they tend to view the results as loss. However, if one is ready to change, they understand that the result is not loss, but a gain of **SPIRITUAL HAPPINESS** and balance. Because when we shift our consciousness to a **SPIRITUAL HAPPINESS** and an understanding of what our purpose is for this current lifetime, we will attract those like-minded souls and more positive situations to us.

It is to our highest and best good to be around people who are happy, positive, accept us for who we are, nonjudgmental, caring, **LOVING**, and **SPIRITUAL**. Too, once we understand and accept the positive life changes, the fear and anxiety of loss goes away. Let me say since my change, I no longer attract dysfunctional people or situations into my life and have **PEACE** and self **LOVE** of myself. As of this writing I have not had a boyfriend in my life for over two years, but do not feel lonely because I have self **LOVE** of myself and I know I am not alone. I have been told in psychic readings that I have seven **ANGELS** around me. I have **GOD**, the universe and my seven **ANGELS** with me 24 hours a day, seven days a week. I also know and trust that they will bring me the right man at the right time to me, and my new friends I have are great people. I also finally understand my family for who they are and have resolved my issues with them in a **SPIRITUAL** realm. (Discussed in the Childhood Abuse chapter). I also find myself giving away and sharing things I feel can help others.

What this book is: It is based on faith and universal **SPIRITUAL** truths that have been channeled to me by my **ANGELS** and guides both in my waking and sleeping state. Those **ANGEL'S** names are Hanna, Jason, Jonas, Leah, Mary, Mennose, Morna, Myrna, Theresa, and Vincent. My goal is to offer the reader information, instead of dictating what people should believe or do. It is up to them if they wish to accept it. There will also be **ANGEL** quotes throughout this book.

What this book is not: It is not an organized religion ego based book that uses bible verses to back up what I say. I was born Catholic and have a rosary hanging from my cars review mirror and that is about as far as it goes for organized religion in my reality. I have never been a fan of organized religion and I was always getting in trouble for not following the religious rules in school.

Back in second grade catechism when I was learning how to do confession in the confessional booth, the nun asked, "tell me child, what are your sins?" and I answered that I have no sins. That went over like an argon balloon and she made me sit in the pitch black of the confessional booth for 30 minutes to think up some sins. It felt more like the tomb of doom because I never did confess any sins. The nun told my dad about what happened when he picked me up, which made my dad mad and I was banished to my room when I arrived home.

These are words from the **ANGEL** Hanna on organized religion:

*"Religion is as only as important as one intends it to be. If you live and preach it, do not use religion for one's own negative agenda. When people invoke the name of **GOD** and his son **JESUS** through religion to the masses, it is to be said with the knowledge of the love that **GOD** and **JESUS** have for all people. **JESUS** has many names and we shall respect those who believe in different religions. It is not good to allow ones egotistical self to be absorbed by the greed of others intentions.*

*"To use religion to misalign others is not of the universal rule of free will. We are free to choose what we want to believe and practice. No one's belief is wrong, yet the religious leaders think they are all right and point to others and say, "you're wrong, you must believe this way." Be not so imposing; let others be their own selves. Remember the **GOD** force is in all of us and that gives us strength to stand within our power. No one is to reach out, grab another, and expect*

them to breech their beliefs. *GOD* is *LOVE*, not fear. So, render not yourself to religion out of fear, but for *LOVE*.

"A closed fear based religion offers only one way to believe-their way. The universe has many more options as *GOD* has only *LOVE*. Religion is good, as long as you do not force it down another person's throat. Every religion thinks it is right and everyone else is wrong. However, no religion is wrong because the believer is right with *GOD*. Some religions are like fishing. Once you take the bait, you are hooked and will have to pay dearly if you want to be saved".

I do not have a degree in theology, or other religious teachings. Religious academic degrees do not matter to *GOD*, the *ANGELS* and the universe. What matters is who we are, what we do while here on earth, and how we help others achieve *SPIRITUAL* growth and knowledge. The true teacher allows *GOD*, the universe and *ANGELS* to channel the truth through them for the **SPIRITUAL** growth of others. The theological academic system of this planet has no authority over who they deem qualified to teach about spirituality and religion. Those systems tend to turn out what they consider academically qualified religious teachers who are ruled by that institutions sometimes egotistical and narrow minded beliefs. These teachers or preachers or priests believe they have the **GOD** given right to judge and condemn others if they do not ascribe or accept these religious leaders belief mindset.

When I was in my spiritually naive early 20's, I joined a 10,000 member southern Baptist church in Phoenix Arizona so I could sing in the choir and play clarinet in the orchestra. The pastor at the time had a PhD in religious theology from a well known religious university in Texas and utilized Dr. in front of his name. I soon discovered from listening to his sermons just how arrogant and ego based his mindset was on his religious views. I heard things such as "shame on you men with thousands of dollars in your saving accounts and you're not sharing it with the church" or "if I happen to come over to your house and open the refrigerator, I better not find any beer in there or I will throw it out" or "for all of you who are not coming to Monday night outreach you better have a good answer why for Jesus when you get to heaven" or "our rich members do not need to give more tithes for **GOD'S** blessings it's our poor members who need to give more tithes for **GOD'S** blessings". The pastor, himself, lived in an expensive home in the Phoenix Mountains, drove a nice car, and wore pricey suits.

For the pastor and his wife's 25th anniversary, a church committee mailed a letter to the members asking for a $25.00 gift to show "our appreciation" for the pastor's service. I did not reply. During a service, the pastor and his wife were told they were to receive an 18K gold flatware set, a brand new Cadillac for the wife, a brand new Rolex for the pastor, and a weeklong ski trip to Vail Colorado with $1200.00 spending money. I was sitting in the choir loft and made an off the cuff comment to the lady sitting next to me, "you know if he was a real man of God, he would sell that stuff and donate it to all to the poor people in our church". The lady agreed with me.

In 1982, the church had a $10 million a year budget and once a year there was a round up barbeque tithing drive and concert with this one famous country western singer who was a church member. A month before the round up, the pastor's sermons were on tithing and he would cherry pick quotations from the Bible to rationalize why the members needed to be good Christian tither's to the church. Two weeks before the round up the church mailed out a detailed budget plan and a tithing pledge form. I noted that $1.7 million dollars was allocated in salaries and retirement funds for the pastor and his six other associates. The form had a choice of tithing 10, 20 or 30% or other amount and then members were to turn in the form at the round up. (I never attended the event and therefore never turned in one). I did go to the concert and was surprised that during the intermission the pastor did a spiel about "how much would you pay for a concert like this?" He then pulled out his checkbook and acted like he was writing a check and expected everyone else to do the same.

I was a member for three years until my night shift government job came along and I had to work weekends so I quit attending. Years later the pastor suddenly resigned from his position in the church due to a supposed affair he was having with some staff member. I never heard anymore about the outcome. The church is still around, but I do not follow what it is doing as it is no longer part of my reality.

Since that time I have learned the Bible today is far removed from the original writings. It has been rewritten over the centuries by the Catholic Church and Anglo Saxon kings with their ego biased slant written into their revisions. The best example is how they make *JESUS* out to be a being void of sexual and earthly desires. Oh please! There was a three hour program aired on the History Channel called The Truth about *JESUS* and how he was born a Jew in the 1st century. The researchers took a human skull from that time period and region and created an image of what *JESUS* would have possibly looked like. He did not look like the white guy images in those religious paintings done by the famous European artists of the middle ages. Also the researchers discovered *JESUS* may have come from a wealthy fishing family and his family may have financed his *SPIRITUAL* pilgrimage. Also the

Bible states *JESUS* was a Rabbi and Rabbi's are required to be married in the conservative Jewish religion.

However, the Bible does serve a *SPIRITUAL* purpose as it does bring people to the *SPIRITUAL* knowledge they need to know at that point in their life. As long as those people trust and have faith in the greater being of *LOVE* and have some idea of what their life purpose is, that is what counts.

Evolved old souls reincarnate all the time into humans such as Gandhi, Mother Teresa, Tesla, Einstein, and the countless lesser known souls who none the less have contributed to the *SPIRITUAL* or technical evolvement of the planet. Regardless of whom the old soul chooses to be born through or where they are born, they know their mission and they will be successful in fulfilling their life purpose.

I am a *SPIRITUALLY* evolved old soul who has reincarnated many lifetimes throughout the centuries of this planet. I chose to return in this lifetime for several reasons. One reason was to overcome the neediness and desperation I have had in romantic relationships with the same souls in several past lifetimes. I am glad to say those issues are rectified and I share how I healed from those issues in these writings.

The other reason is that I still have more to contribute to the *SPIRITUAL* growth of this planet. It has not been an easy life for me as the negative energies and emotions of the unenlightened souls around me were constantly invading my personal space creating anxiety, sadness, anger and unhappiness. This would cause me to question my choice of returning and my *ANGELS* and guides sensing those negative feelings filled my being with *LOVE* and *HAPPINESS* so I could carry on despite this planet of craziness.

Universal Rules

The following is the Universal Rules that the *ENLIGHTENED SOUL* knows, understands and follows. These are channeled in from my *ANGELS* and are not something I made up. When reading these rules, they seem like common sense, yet many people do not follow them. To understand and accept these rules requires letting go of negative ego. That can be challenging especially when dealing with difficult family members, friends, our bosses or people we judge as mean, jerks, idiots, sinners or evil. To live by these Universal Rules will bring **GOD'S** blessings of **PEACE** and **HAPPINESS**, a better understanding of us and others, and a harmonious thought process and mindset.

1. *Let others be who they are and respect the beliefs and lifestyles of all souls.* Everyone has their reasons for being on earth and is responsible for their lessons. We are not to judge, condemn, control or try to change a person.
2. *Impose not our will upon others.* Your will is energy and when someone forces their will upon another person, it can make them sick.
3. *PRAYERS are to be pure, not intrusive.* For example, if a staunch Baptist thinks that someone is living in sin and **PRAYS** that they need to turn back to **GOD** that is being intrusive. This intrusiveness is negative energy and can make the person ill we are **PRAYING** for. When we **PRAY**, we are to **PRAY** that GOD either helps, or **LOVES** or guides the person for their highest and best good.
4. *We chose our parents, siblings, friends and anyone else with whom we are to interact with, because nothing is coincidental, all is intentionally planned and agreed upon.*
5. *There is no sin, just evil creating detours.* Organized religion is really big on people committing sins. The universe does not recognize sin, as there is no such thing. When a person allows the negative energy of the planet to overtake them and they become evil and or lost, they create a detour from their life's mission.
6. *We are free to choose our method of passing over from our life on earth, but not by suicide.* Explained in 2.1 Planning our Earth Life on the Other Side.
7. *We are not to blame others for what we have chosen.* We are responsible for all our decisions.
8. *Remember that we cannot change our past. What was, was, and what will be in our future is what we need to focus on.*
9. *Focus on the present and live in the now. We are to enjoy the moment and relish in what we have before we can move on to the future.*
10. *We are to stand in our own power to overtake the negativity around us.*

11. *We MANIFEST our life by our words, thoughts and actions, be they positive or negative. So, if we say it enough, we will believe it. When we believe it; we will MANIFEST it.*
12. *GOD will provide what is needed for our lessons.*
13. *We will repeat the same lessons until we learn and understand.*
14. *We are born into this world with what talents we bring. It is the lessons that are waiting.*
15. *We are to forgive so as not to let anger consume us.* Anger kills, and manes the soul body and mind.

Love is....

Listening instead of giving your biased opinion.

Chapter 1: LIVING THE HAPPY LIFE

1.1 How the SPIRITUAL Universe Operates

ANGEL quote: *"We think we know perfection but many times our idea of perfection is ego driven. There is perfection in all that is created by **GOD**; we only have to look past the ego. Let not your mind trap your thoughts of despair. Hear what we say. You are free of all that may hinder you. Ask it is yours. Rest and sleep, do not worry; let your mind go and be free to feel **LOVE**. Do not allow others to steal your thoughts away. Keep within **LOVE** and also let go to share your **LOVE** and life of joy".*

We can live a happy life despite what our surroundings are. We can transform ourselves into **SPIRITUALLY** productive beings whose egos do not interfere with our learning and **HAPPINESS**. We do not have to be limited by the negative and closed minded programming that has been ingrained into our brains from childhood to our current time. We can learn how to tap into the unlimited knowledge that the universe has to offer, if we chose to accept it. Tapping in is done by **PRAYING** to **GOD** and our **ANGELS** to show and lead us to the knowledge we need to live a more happy and **SPIRITUAL** life. Information may come in bursts of inspiration or in the dream state. Inspiration is not ego based and does not go away; it will gnaw at us until we follow it.

There is also the Akashic hall of records that contains the past life records of all souls in the universe. When a person learns to access and open their records, they learn how their past lives affect their current incarnation. However, this book does not cover how to access your own records as there are books already written on this topic.

Think how wonderful it would be if all humans were highly **SPIRITUAL** evolved citizens of earth. There would be no wars. Not as many people would be as interested in designer clothes, cars, expensive houses and having the newest and greatest electronic gadgets of the day. We would not be back stabbing people to get ahead, we would be more honest and kinder towards others, take better care of ourselves, obesity would not be the problem it is today, we would not be in the financial mess we are, we would not be cheating on our spouses, stealing from others, and child and domestic abuse would not exist. Starvation and hunger would not be as wide spread. But to accomplish this would require a world wide effort from everyone to change. Not an easy task to accomplish, but with **PRAYER** and sending **LOVE** out into the world maybe we can come close to it.

However, the earth is a large third dimensional classroom of free wills and earthly temptations with different learning situations and that is why not everyone is highly evolved **SPIRITUAL** beings. That is also why abuse, hunger, illness, stealing, lying, killing and other crimes exist.

Then there are those people known as the revolving door souls who are keep coming back but are not **SPIRITUALLY** evolving. These are the people we old souls know as materialistic, closed minded, insecure, self-centered, caught up in the drama of the world, complainers, takers, jealous of who we are, and do not feel comfortable being around us.

Three things about revolving door souls are:

1) They cannot handle the evolved energy of the old soul if they are not ready to evolve themselves.
2) No matter how old they are chronologically, if they do not **SPIRITUALLY** evolve they will be the same emotionally throughout their lives.
3) Ego maturity does not equate to **SPIRITUAL** maturity. People can act and appear to be mature, but still have a selfish based ego that is not **SPIRITUALLY** mature.

Our earth is here to help teach us to become **LOVING** and **SPIRITUAL** beings. The tuition is birth, the length of our education is determined how much we need to learn and experience to rectify our negative karma and the degree is the next step in our **SPIRITUAL** development. This **SPIRITUAL** development is our key to progressing to the next level on the other side.

I also want to note that sometimes souls return to earth who do not have heavy karma to rectify, but just return to enjoy life. They may still have lessons to learn, but their lives are fun, happy and blessed. These are the blessed people who seem to attract money and live the life of Riley, have great friends, great kids and spouses and go through life without any major tragedies.

1.2 Programming

During the nine months in the womb our souls come and go as needed. The reason is that we are being prepared and conditioned mentally to survive on planet earth. Because of this acclimation, when we are born our souls, minds and bodies are pure. However, this ends rather quickly if we are born into an un*LOVING* and abusive situation. Depending on what we have chosen as our life mission, our lives can be short. That is why two month old babies die. Maybe their purpose was to rectify for a killing they did in a past lifetime. Maybe the baby was abusive to the current parents in a past lifetime and the baby rectified his/her negative karma by allowing the parents to be the abuser. Whatever the reason, the baby made the choice to go through the abuse. This may be a difficult concept to accept, but it is a universal truth; we chose and plan out what we will be doing on earth.

If we are born into **LOVING** families our purity only lasts until the child tells mommy or daddy they are talking to their friends (**ANGELS** or **GOD**), and the parents tell the child that is not a good thing and to stop. As a result the child's crown chakra shuts down. If the child continues to talk or see things, then the parents may become concerned that their child is mentally ill and takes them for counseling. If the parents happen to be wise and open minded, they will know the difference between mental illness and a **SPIRITUAL** child. Unfortunately, most parents themselves are **SPIRITUALLY** shut down.

A chakra is an energy point in our body and can cause problems if blocked. The body has seven chakras located in different areas, they are: *Crown*: top of the head where we receive **SPIRITUAL** information. *Third Eye*: forehead where we can see **SPIRITS**. *Throat and heart*: If blocked can cause throat and heart illnesses. *Solar plexus*: slightly above the navel and can cause stomach problems if blocked. *Sacral*: slightly below the navel and can cause indigestion if blocked. *Root*: base of spine which can cause sexual problems, disease or illness if blocked. (There is a web site listed in the Appendix for more information).

Our brain is like a computer that is programmed with *SPIRITUAL*, positive or negative programming. The programming that is hard wired into our brain is what keeps us where we are at any point in our lives. We were programmed from birth by our parents and grandparents, teachers, media and our peers. Those programs is what causes us to be either *LOVING*, happy, sad, anxiety ridden, negative, angry, abusive to others and our children, mistrustful, and just plain ornery.

If we happen to be happy and *SPIRITUAL*, then our bodies, mind and soul will run without a lot of crashes. However, if we have negative programming, then our bodies circuitry (chakras) with be fought with blockages causing illnesses, obesity, un*HAPPINESS*, discontent, and money and family problems. Therefore, since programming is the problem, blaming everyone else is not going to solve our problems. Even in this so called period of enlightenment, we as souls are still bombarded with negativity and egotistical tenets of religious and governmental rhetoric. We are spoon fed garbage in order to keep the sheep in line so they do not question the status quo or rise up in mass protest.

The programming we received depended upon the environment we lived in and what hard wired programs our caretakers downloaded into us. There are basically only two types of childhood environments we all grew up in; either an *LOVING* or un*LOVING* one.

In the stable and *LOVING* environment we were *LOVED*, had parents, grandparents and others who *LOVED* us. They nourished our minds, they cheered us on, they believed in us and wanted to see us succeed and be happy. *GOD*, religion and going to church may have been a large part of our lives. We grew up into well adjusted happy adults because of positive and *LOVING* programming that made our family's life good.

In the chaotic and un*LOVING* environment, it was during the crucial years as a child when we needed *LOVE* to flourish and grow emotionally; we did not receive it. We were ignored, pushed aside, made to feel worthless, or abused. We were starved for *LOVE*. Maybe once in awhile we got a meager scrap of *LOVE* and gobbled it up like six starved Dobermans fighting over one can of dog food. Then we waited desperately for the next morsel of **LOVE**. Sometimes we were tricked into thinking we were going to get **LOVE** but instead it was sporadic and hence we developed mistrust towards our caretakers. We built up our defenses and their names were fear, desperation and neediness and they became our constant companion and they never went away. They followed us into adulthood and became the same dog and pony show on the same channel we replayed over and over again.

So, whatever the environment, there is always room for improvement. The first step in healing the mind, body, and soul is to let go of any negative programming by turning it over to **GOD** and **PRAYING**. Say this **PRAYER** for each blockage that we feel is hindering us from being happy and at **PEACE** with ourselves.

"My dear GOD, please take away these negative blockages that are hindering and stopping me from achieving a happy life of LOVE, belonging and success. I ask that you fill my heart, mind and soul with your LOVE instead. I thank you and LOVE you my dear GOD. Amen".

Additional steps will be introduced that will continue the **SPIRITUAL** healing process. However, if the healing methods in this book are not resounding with your belief system, please find the right venue that will work for you. The goal is to be a happy, **LOVING** and positive person.

Below is another **PRAYER** to help release negative programming that can be said in the morning and evening. It can be said in the shower, during shaving, drinking the first cup of coffee, or the time between the first rings of the alarm clock to the snoozer or before falling asleep.

"Dear GOD and my ANGELS. I ask you to take away the negativity from my being. I am releasing all my sadness, anger, fear, and mistrust to you. Please help me to let go of the need to control everything. I ask your help in loving others instead of criticizing them by filling my heart, mind and soul with your LOVE. I thank you and I LOVE you my dear GOD and ANGELS. Amen".

Remember, words are energy and our words in **PRAYER** transcend our consciousness to a higher vibration of **LOVE**.

Chapter 2 WE CHOOSE TO BE BORN

2.1 Planning Our Earth Life on the Other Side

To understand why we are here on earth requires letting go of the preconceived notions that we have been told by others, the media and organized religion.

One dogma that some religions teach is that we only live one life and there is no such thing as reincarnation. However, if that were true then everyone would choose to live charmed lives. No one would choose to live in poverty, or be hungry, or abused or sick. Well hate to bust the bark of dogma, but life is not a one shot deal; it offers many lifetimes for learning.

Choice is just not something that happens on earth; choice is all encompassing. It extends beyond the earth; it is universal. We choose and plan what we will do before we are born. We choose what our *SPIRITUAL* lessons will be on earth for our *SPIRITUAL* evolvement. The success of those lessons will determine if we ascend to the next *SPIRITUAL* level when we pass over. Choice never ends and we chose the life we are living now.

On the other side, it is separated into two different dimensions; our dream dimension and the dimension to which we pass over to a.k.a. heaven. When we dream we have a silver cord that keeps our souls attached to our bodies. If we are **SPIRITUALLY** advanced souls, we may occasionally get a glimpse of the other side where we go when we pass over, but cannot yet visit. The souls who have passed over can come over into the dream world and go back, but we cannot go over to them.

During the lifetime planning stage on the other side, we plan how we will die. After death a person goes through a life review and an adjustment period. Depending upon what the **SPIRITUAL** evolvement of the soul was at death that is where they will go on the other side. A soul cannot advance to a higher level if they did not learn the lessons they were suppose to while on earth.

As we reach higher **SPIRITUAL** realms, we gain more responsibility in helping and teaching the souls in the lower realms with their lessons. And, interestingly, if we think classroom learning will be the same on the other side with desks, blackboards, being lectured and taking notes that is what our experience will be. Myself, when I have dreams of being in the traditional classroom, I am there to help the other students. When I am learning something new it is interactive, visual and not in the classroom setting.

No matter how negative or evil a soul is, they are still given chance after chance to learn. They are allowed to keep returning to earth until that soul demonstrates they are not learning or getting it. Then they have the opportunity to learn on the other side at their **SPIRITUAL** level.

There are also collective souls that come as one to do a mass learning such as despots like Hitler, Pol Pot, Stalin, etc. If these souls were born as individuals then their negative energy would be tenfold. One might ask why did **GOD** even let these horrible and evil people be born. The reason is that according to the universe every soul is entitled to return as many times as they need to learn their lessons.

When we choose to reincarnate, we are not allowed to end our life contract early by suicide. When a person commits suicide, be it personal choice or with the intent to kill others, the person ends up walking the earth in a different dimension. They think they are alive, and no one hears or sees them as their classroom is feeling and experiencing the pain, sorrow, hate, and sadness they created. This is known as limbo in the Catholic religion. These souls are truly sorry for what they did after the fact, but they are going nowhere fast as the universe will not allowed them to pass over. They are in constant penance and **PRAYER** to whoever their **GOD** is for forgiveness. When the soul is done learning their lessons they move on to the other side where they have to be reborn to complete their contract. We should pray for anyone we know who commits suicide that **GOD** and the universe will forgive them and let them move on so they can return to complete their life contract.

We all hear people will say, "Well I didn't choose to be born and definitely did not choose my family". But yes, we did choose our parents, brothers, sisters, and friends and planned how we would live and interact with them on the earth. We have been with the same family members in past lifetimes and will continue reincarnating with them until we are done learning what we need to with them. We will switch roles in different lifetimes in order to experience what we need for **SPIRITUAL** growth and to rectify our negative karma. However, the family or friend that chooses their role may not fulfill their contract with us. They forget their purpose despite their inner voice, intuition and being placed into several situations that are intended to wake up their subconscious memory into action.

Here is example of my interaction with a family member in a past life time in the Middle East. I was married to a well to do man who had made a personal fortune. His nuclear family was not that well off and was jealous of my then husband's success and me because I would be the one to inherit the money. My husband's family conspired to gain control of the money and went to the town or village caliph (a religious leader), who was my now ex brother in law in this life time, to plead their case. Whatever the reason, the caliph sided with the family and ordered that my husband and my hands be cut off. Of course, we could not work and his family took over our estate and kicked us to the curb. (These dynamics still occur in many families today).

In this life time my ex brother in law was not that close to me. He owns a profitable tile business and was generous in spending money on my son and daughter on things such as karate lessons, starting a baseball card collection and paying off my daughter's school tuition and helping my grandchildren. These actions indirectly were his way of rectifying the negative karma towards me.

We all come from different **SPIRITUAL** levels on the other side to earth; the place of both positive and negative diverse learning opportunities. On the other side there is not the negativity the earth has. For example on the other side a lesson in poverty is theoretical; the student will not experience actual poverty. When the student is done with class they do not go back to a poverty living situation and thus takes much longer to complete a lesson. But on the earth we can experience poverty and in a short time we can understand the ramifications of having no job and money, being hungry, homeless, and physically or mentally ill from poverty.

Another aspect is on earth we learn lessons quicker because time moves quicker here than on the other side. For example, when I was 45 years old, during a reading the psychic stated that there was a passed over 12 year boy standing to my right side. The boy was a brother of my boyfriend at the time. The boyfriend had found his then six month old brother dead of SIDS in the crib and carried that guilt into adulthood. The boy was relating the message that my boyfriend was to let go of the guilt and that it was not his fault. The age ratio was 3.7 earth years to one other side year which was figured by dividing 12 into 45.

When we pass over in death, we are acclimated back to the positive energy of the other side. We have a life review of what we did to others, learned and accomplished. If we did not complete the lessons or feel we need more lesson time then we start planning our next earth adventure. During the planning there is not a fear factor that something may go wrong or we will fail because our plans our perfect.

We also plan out our financial provisions, and provide what we will need to complete our earthly lessons. In other words; we will be without. However, for the majority of us, once we return and become acclimated and get drawn into the negative earth energy, we turn into worry warts as adults. Instead of trusting **GOD**, our **ANGELS**, and the universe we worry that if we do not get an education to get a good job in order to pay the bills, the kid's education and buy the materialist things we need, we will end up broke and homeless. Worrying is energy and the type of worry your ego is creating will **MANIFEST** itself. Worry overrides what we planned out. So let go of the worry because the plans we made are perfect and we will be provided for.

2.2 Children

*The enlightened parent knows it is wise to **LOVE**, be patient, and take the time to teach a child from birth, then to wait till they are a rebellious teenager to start. And it is easier to **LOVE** and be kind to a child from birth than to heal an abused adult.*

The role of children trumps the role of the parent as the child has all the power when it comes to deciding who the parents will be and what lessons they want to learn and experience. The parental roles are to keep the child safe, fed, housed, clothed and provide the proper education. Parents are to be open-minded in order to see what the child's talents are and encourage them to succeed in what they are to do. We are not to dictate what we think the child should grow up to be by living our dreams through them or fulfilling a family legacy or expecting the child to live up to our expectations. Parents are the caretakers of the children of **GOD**, not the owner.

Those soon to be children of ours also have the power to decide if they do not want to follow through with the birth contract. *Everything is planned, nothing is by accident.* If they decide not to, the result is miscarriages, stillbirths, abortions and SIDS. While the fetus is in the womb, the soul can come and go as it pleases. During this time the soul has the option if they want to continue or end the birth contract. That is the risk we as parents take when we decide to have children; the child has the right to not go through with the birth contract. Just as we as women have the right to change our mind and not bear the number of children we agreed upon on the other side.

And then there are those children who seem to be wise beyond their years. These children are usually old souls who know their mission which requires a strong sense of self from the start. Sometimes a child ends up being a pseudo parent in a dysfunctional household. This is a complex situation with many factors. Maybe the child has to experience the same role they did to the parent in a previous lifetime. Or maybe the parent chose to learn how to overcome dependency, or to care for others or to let go of being selfish or whatever their reason. Sometimes, despite the parents good intentions, once on earth, they cannot overcome those fear based emotions and they fall prey to drugs, alcohol or illness. Even though the wise child is left holding the bag, they innately know that it is not their fault and come to terms with the situation and make **PEACE** within their soul.

Abortion is a learning situation that is decided and agreed upon by both the mother and the child. For example, a child may need to work through some karma with the mother, but does not want to go through with their birth contract. When the abortion is being done, the soul can choose to leave or go through the experience. The universal view of abortion is that it is not like murdering a person that is living outside the womb. When we are living outside the womb, our souls stay here with us until after we die; they cannot just exit the body at will as they can in womb. Thus when you murder a person outside the womb, it creates a negative imbalance and karma, and we also end up going to prison on top of that.

As far as resolving karma through abortion, let us say the child killed the mother in another lifetime and instead of the child being born and then the mother killing the child, the baby's soul is allowing the abortion to rectify the karma. After all women do not go to prison for having an abortion. And we are not to judge those who decide upon having an abortion--it is their decision according to what their life mission and fulfillment of karma is.

Don't judge others....

Until you've walked a mile in their shoes.

Miscarriage is another way the soul cancels the birth contract or to learn a lesson. Of course, science has the explanation that miscarriages happen because the fetus is genetically defective. However, many children are born with damaged genetic systems.

Then there are the women who carry a fetus to full term without any problem and then have a stillborn child. This is because a soul has the right to cancel the birth contract any time before birth. Also, it could be another lesson or karma that the mother and the child's soul need to complete. A baby also has a small time frame to cancel the life contract after they are born and SIDS is one way the baby chooses to leave.

When people end up being cruel, abusive or killing their kids, they may be denied having children in future lifetimes. These are the women who desperately want kids, but cannot conceive or carry a fetus to full term due to infertility, sexual disease or some other medical problem. Then they spend thousands of dollars to conceive, but still do not. Then try to adopt, but encounter endless roadblocks that keep them from achieving that goal.

Kids cry, are fussy, have temper tantrums, are moody, and temperamental. Their brains develop from the back occipital lobe to frontal lobe. The frontal lobe is where rational thought or executive functioning occurs. The frontal lobe is not developed until around the age of 22 and therefore kids tend not to think things through. That is why, for example, a promising high school senior who is an A+ student, has a scholarship to an Ivy League school, and excels in sports, will out of the clear blue shoplift, drink and drive, or end up dead from doing a stupid stunt. It is because they literally have occasional short circuits or brain farts.

That is why when we get angry at our children and start yelling, screaming and demanding to know why they did it; they answer "I don't know", and give us a blank stare. Their spur of the moment action was not planned out; it just happened. Never assume "my child is too smart to do anything foolish to ruin his/her life. They have too much promise". As parents, it is an ongoing thing that we must always reiterate with our **LOVING** intent by teaching the consequences of not thinking things through.

Yelling, screaming, threats, and arguing is a losing battle and never solves a single problem and is only going to make the situation worse. If we had parents that yelled, screamed and hit us how did we feel? Did we think it worked? For those who say yes, then these may be the reasons why:

1. We believe that we deserved to be yelled and screamed at and whipped because we believe that we were a bad kid that caused our parents all kinds of problems.
2. We have no patience and get angry very easily and rationalize that it got results when our parents did it and it works for us.
3. We don't know any other way to discipline a child and find it easier to scream, yell and hit instead of taking the time to handle the situation with patience.

4. The child's behavior subconsciously reminds us of how un**LOVED** and misunderstood we felt for something we may not have had any control over or did not even do.

5. We blame our yelling, screaming and hitting on being tired, frustrated that the kids are a burden on our finances, not respecting or listening to us, embarrassing us in front of our friends, disobeying and back talking us, and the countless other excuses that we can think of to rationalize our lack of control and patience.

Hitting our children is never acceptable as it only teaches the child that is the way you solve problems.

If we have no patience; then we need to **PRAY** to **GOD** for it. However, we may think, easier said than done. Here is the thing, anger is like pain. If a person has an injury and is taking pain medication, the reason is to take away the pain or keep it at an acceptable level. If we do not take the pain medication regularly then the pain will keep increasing until it becomes unbearable and out of control. So, **PRAY** every day to **GOD** for patience and understanding for when a situation crops up we can control the anger to avoid the escalation into uncontrollable screaming, yelling and or hitting.

"Dear GOD, give me patience in my heart now that I will not do anything in anger and frustration. I need your LOVE within me to keep me focused on understanding the situation at hand. Thank you and amen".

When we stay in control and practice patience, we are teaching our child that this works. It will keep us focused and help solve the problem at hand.

Also, as parents we can either go overboard with or not care enough about our children. Our children are special to us, their grandparents, uncles, aunts, brothers and sisters. We might think our children are the smartest, prettiest, handsomest, the best at sports, and other activities. Our best friends and the school may think so too. *However, other people outside that group will not view our child as special*.

Other people will avoid us if we constantly flaunt our wonderful child's achievements in their faces every time we see them. People may give us lip service but the fact is they do not care if our children win awards at school sports day, made the cheer squad or marching band at school, made the swimming team, got all A's on their report card, or got accepted into Harvard, etc. Other people think their kids are just as great and will boast about it right back at us.

Then there are the parent(s) who do not kept control of their children in public. When my sisters and I were small, my mom would let us wander unsupervised in the store while she shopped. My one sister was always stealing gum and candy and shoving it inside her clothes. I remember the store manager approaching my mom about it and a body search of my sister would ensue. My mom would become embarrassed and angrily hiss at us when we were hurried out of the store, "you damn bratty kids, wait till you're dad gets home". Of course, she would not punish us, but instead when we returned home from the store we would all run back outside and play. When my dad got home, she would wait till we were all eating dinner at the table to say "guess what Linda did today in the store" and she proceeded to expound on the details. Of course, my dad would yell and spank my sister and we would all end up in our rooms.

People will despise the parent(s) who have kids that are bullies and will sue us if our child causes damage to their children and property. Children learn bullying from their bully parents words, actions and behaviors at home. Parent(s) that beat their children with their hands, belts or objects teach children it is okay to hit others in response to anger. Or the parent(s) who gossips, degrades, insults and or makes fun of their friends or neighbors behind closed doors. And yes, our children are listening when we don't think they are. "Ron's wife looks like a cheap slut with those clothes she wears. She must really be good in the sack because it costs a lot of money to look cheap like that!". "I don't like that woman, she is such a bore". "We don't associate with the Jones; she's a raging alcoholic and her husband is a real jerk. I feel sorry for those kids". "Tom's cheap, that's why they never have a new car or do anything".

Of course, there are the children who people refer to as "just pure evil". These are the kids who kill the parents or do other actions just as bad. Again, this is planned out before we are born, or it is a karmatic situation to be resolved. We have to give our permission to allow the dynamics that occur between another soul and us to be carried out on earth. It is not an unplanned and accidental situation.

The way to survive others negativity and raise loving children is to teach our children to have a healthy respect for others. This is accomplished by **LOVING** our children and spending as much time with them as we can and teaching them about respect, being kind to others, using good manners and acceptable behavior. We should also **PRAY** that **GOD** guides us in raising our children to be happy, **LOVING** and productive adults. Our children have the same rights to live their life as we do instead of us controlling and dictating our children. We are responsible for guiding and setting examples, and giving them abundant **LOVE** and in return **GOD** shall bless all.

2.3 Money is Not the Root of All Evil

Money is a necessity and there is no way around it. As said before depending upon the lessons a person needs to learn, we planned how we would be provided for on earth. The universe then sends those provisions we need to survive and fulfill our lessons.

These lessons might be the need to learn to stop worshiping money and obtaining it at the expense of others. Maybe a person needs to experience living in poverty because they were a con artist in a past life time. They might be a wealthy person who is to share their wealth and will effortlessly **MANIFEST** and attract money to them. We may have to work very hard to earn every dollar we obtain. Maybe a person will win a large sum of money in order to learn how to be a good steward of the money. Whatever the reasons, **GOD**, our **ANGELS,** and the universe will make sure we receive what we need. That is why we should be thankful every day for what they have provided to us.

Money is energy and if we create negative energy with money in the form of worry, greed and selfishness, the negative energy will **MANIFEST** at our expense. Cheating, lying and stealing may bring temporary wealth but then the thief will lose it somewhere later on in their life. The following is an example about how a man did not learn his lesson about greed and it caught up to him in this lifetime.

Joe was a self centered, narcissist who worked as an engineer who cared more for money than his pregnant wife, Mary. Joe had just left Mary for another woman, Jayne, he met twelve days earlier on a group camping trip. The day Joe left Mary, he and Jayne went to the bank and withdrew $50,000.00 from Joe's joint bank account he had with Mary. His rationale was that since he made $120,000.00 a year and the wife had been in nursing school and only working part time, it was his money.

The following day when Mary was at work, Joe drove Jayne's pickup truck to the house he and Mary owned together. There he removed the TV, stereo, computer, some furniture, CDs, coins and saving bonds. Joe's rationale was that since he had paid for those items, they were his. A neighbor had called Mary at work and Mary arrived at the house as Joe was getting in the truck. Mary got out of her car, running towards the truck yelling for Joe to stop. As Joe drove off, Mary then managed to scratch the trucks paint with her car keys. Jayne than filed an insurance claim against Mary for damages. Joe and Jayne then moved into Joe's childhood home he had purchased from his parents. Joe then signed over the other house to Mary to avoid making payments. Joe never reimbursed Mary for what he took.

When Mary and Joes baby was born, Joe did not attend the birth. Jayne began to have a fit when Joe was court ordered to pay child support. Ten years later, Joe finally married Jayne but it ended in divorce after five years and Jayne received a $75,000.00 lump sum. Then Joe was demoted in his job and his pay was decreased from $65.00 an hour to $40.00 an hour, his parents died and he obtained a large inheritance.

After the divorce Joe bought another house and married a gold digger who claimed she had a lot of money. She and her adult son moved into the house and managed to con Joe out of the inheritance. When Joe discovered the con job, he filed for divorce. A nasty divorce fight ensued and Joe had to sell his house to pay the legal fees. Then his pay was cut to $30.00 an hour and he filed bankruptcy. Two months later Joe found another woman who fell for his sob story about the bitches in his life who ripped him off and she moved in two weeks after meeting him.

The moral of the above example is if we are negative and selfish instead of being honest and wise stewards of our money, we will **MANIFEST** what we project out to the universe. If we tell people that "I don't have the money, I can't afford that, I may lose it all tomorrow, I have to save my money, I just can't give it away", the universe hears those words and **MANIFESTS** it. If we understand and project that **GOD** and the universe is taking care of us, and let go of the fear and worry, we live a happy and prosperous life.

It is okay to have money and to be wealthy. Money does not have to be elusive, or evil; money **LOVES** to come to those who **LOVE** to have it. **LOVING** money is not the same as worshiping money. We should **LOVE** that money is used for the betterment of ourselves and others. Do not chase money just for the sake of chasing it and then hoard it, because we are meant to keep the flow going. **PRAYING** to **GOD** and our **ANGELS** for guidance in career and education will help us to achieve our goals and needs.

Be honest and fair with money and let go of the fear of not having money. Proclaim *"I am wealthy, I am wealthy"* over and over. Be a good steward of what we do have; do not waste it, but spend and give it away wisely. Thank the good Lord everyday for providing us with it. We should protect our money, bank accounts, savings, stocks, bonds and any other wealth with the white light of **GOD's LOVE**.

Another aspect is that not everyone will have money because of what the person planned for themselves on the other side. That is why there is abject poverty all over the world. Poverty and starvation are lessons that the soul chooses to live in; it is not an accidental situation. For those who are not living in poverty and starvation, it gives us the opportunity to share our **ABUNDANCE**. We as souls, at one time or another will probably choose to live in poverty as it reaps great rewards in our soul growth and deeper appreciation of the gifts the universe and planet earth provides and bestows upon us.

If a person is having a problem letting go of money worries and cannot trust that they planned for being taken care of, here is what can be done: Write out a list of the monetary issues that are causing us worry and that we think about constantly. Then go through each item on the list saying **"I do**

not need this worry/problem". Next ask *GOD* to take that worry/problem out of our mind, soul, and body. Then ask *GOD* to show us how the universe has taken care of this worry/problem. Then thank the Lord and say I *LOVE* you.

Do this anytime those worrisome thoughts sneak back into our mind. We may find ourselves doing it frequently. The answer on how the worry/problem may be resolved may come as a flash of inspiration on how to make some money, or money may unexpectedly show up. Or it *MANIFESTS* in additional work hours at our job. Have an open mind to receiving the gifts, answers and opportunities bestowed upon us. Too, we may not have much, but what we got is what we need and that is blessings enough for us.

2.4 When I win the Lottery

We would all like to win the lottery as it is easy to spend and give away money we do not have to work for or is someone else's. We all have those plans ready to implement if we do. We would pay off the credit card bills, buy a new car, buy a new house, start a business, travel around the world on a cruise liner, help our family, or give money to charity or any number of things; all good intentions.

Here is how the universe looks at winning money. If we want the flow of money to come to us, we have to be willing to keep the flow going. This means showing the universe that we believe we are worthy and deserving of receiving money by willingly doing all those good intentions today. We are rewarded according to what we give away freely without expecting anything in return. (I know because it works for me!)

Want to pay off credit card bills? Then find ways to cut down on spending to pay off the credit card.

Want a new car or a new house? If possible, try working extra overtime at the job, or obtain a second job or find a way to make extra money that can be saved up for a new car or new house.

Start a business? Sit down and draw up a five year business plan complete with financing, equipment, the employees one will need, and all the bells and whistles.

Go around the world? Start taking small inexpensive trips around where you live. This shows we want to travel.

Help my family and give to charity. I figured while I was waiting for that large lottery winning to come my way, I started giving money to help my daughter that was already in my bank account. Of course, I buy a weekly lottery ticket and tell the universe it is the winner, but I still have not won the big jackpot. However, I receive blessings in many other areas all the time.

2.5 Universal Energy

Angel Quote: "LOVE is energy. When our entire being is all LOVE, our soul, mind and body is at PEACE. That PEACE is LOVING energy that heals others. Open your chakras through the soul and let your LOVING and positive energies flow out from you to others".

Our voice, intentions, emotions, thoughts and actions are all energy and permeate whatever we handle, touch or speak to. We are to respect our energy and where it is directed. It takes practice through mantras and *PRAYERS* to use our energy wisely and for our highest and best good.

If we hate where live, it will crumble. If we hate what we do it will be unproductive. If we hate others and speak badly of them; then we will get that energy we spew out 100 fold back to us. When we say things such as "I don't have it, nothing is free, and someone has to pay for it and I don't have this or that" the universe will reward us accordingly which equates to nothing. Instead if we speak the words, "I am worthy and entitled to all the riches of the universe and I am constantly being rewarded abundantly", this results in what we believe.

We are to embrace and give thanks to *GOD* for those gifts of *LOVE*, *KINDNESS*, *HAPPINESS*, food, our job, the roof over our heads, and good health that are bestowed upon us so they shall flourish. When we receive the *ABUNDANCE* of money, we are not to put materialistic things first over our *LOVED* ones. Nor do we waste that money on buying things to satisfy our egos need to keep up with the Joneses. The end result is usually loss and a hard lesson. Example: In the years before the 2007 housing crash, there were all those people who had to have that overinflated big priced house and financed it with subprime loans. Then they maxed out their several different credit cards to furnish the house. Then they had to have a new car, while still paying off school loans. And even though both people were living paycheck to paycheck they had good jobs and were making it. Then the housing bubble bust, jobs were gone and people lost all their prized possessions. A hard lesson of how destructive greed and ego is.

Food is another area where our energies are absorbed. If a person hates cooking for themselves, their family or others, their negative energy will permeate the food and it tends to taste bad. My mother hated to cook and would be drunk when preparing dinner and I use to get physically ill from eating some of her dishes. When my dad would occasionally cook, he seemed to enjoy the task and involved my sisters and I and the food tasted great. My sisters and I would constantly beg him to cook and he said, "No that's your mother job, let her do it".

I believe food is a living energy and I tell the food I *LOVE* and thank it when preparing a meal. As a result, my dishes taste as good as what I have eaten in five star restaurants. When I told my sister about my thoughts on this subject, she retorted, "So if someone is cooking with arsenic, then they are going to make it safe to eat by *LOVING* it? Do you know how ridiculous what you are saying sounds? It makes no sense". I felt her comment probably stemmed from that since she had a lifetime of working experience in various restaurants and I did not, I had no idea what I was talking about and should not be writing about food.

Regardless of what negative comments are said to us, anything we want that is positive and beneficial; visualize it, write it down and feel the good emotions that go with it. Then send out the good energies and *PRAYERS* to the universe to *MANIFEST* its being.

2.6 Our Health

As with everything else, we plan on the other side how health will play in our lives. The responsible soul knows that according to the rules of karma, if we inflicted pain upon another person's body in a past lifetime causing either physical or mental damage; we must pay for that pain in a future lifetime. Examples such as if we were a wife or child beater and caused bruising, broken bones, left scars, or permanent bodily damage on our victim; in a future lifetime we might have arthritis, kidney failure, cancer, or a poor immune system. Or a person we abused in one lifetime may be born as our child with a genetic disease that will require us to be the selfless caretaker. Or if in a past lifetime we were a person who conned money from desperate sick people in exchange for the promise that we would cure their disease but did nothing. In this lifetime we might suffer from a disease or condition where we cannot earn a living and live in poverty or be forced to file medical bankruptcy due to a health condition.

Our good health is a positive karmatic reward for being kind and not hurting others in past lifetimes. That is why some people will not have health problems throughout their lifetime. These are the people who do not get heart disease, high blood pressure, strokes, type II diabetes, become obese or any other chronic condition.

Of course the choices of how we want to repay our karmatic health debt are many. A soul may chose to go through the experience of being born with a genetic disease like cancer to teach others to be advocates for research. That is why a three year old child with cancer seems to be wise beyond their years.

A soul may use the dominant and recessive genes that will cause disease. If a group of souls want to experience a certain dominant genetic disease such as breast cancer, they may all be born into the same family.

I have been told, that there is a history of heart disease in my family brought on by bad diets and smoking. At age 55, my dad's carotid arteries were 98% and 20% blocked, respectively and he had to undergo angioplasty. My uncle had a heart attack in his 60's from a long term constant daily diet of fast food. My grandfather was diagnosed with heart disease in his 50's. My grandmother had congestive heart failure. However, this life time is not destined for me to suffer chronic or devasting disease. What occurred to my family members is due to what they needed to rectify their negative karmatic debts.

A soul may need to overcome an addiction such as gluttony, drug use, smoking, or drinking that killed them in a past life time. However, if they return and lose the addiction battle again, a disease may result from it.

We can unintentionally catch a disease or become sick when someone sneezes on us, or we eat contaminated food, or are exposed to disease producing carcinogens without our knowledge. We cannot foresee all unintentional disease states that occur and sometimes kills people. However, if we are healthy we usually overcome the disease. We are also supposed to protect ourselves by getting the preventative vaccinations; as **GOD** gave the information to the scientists to create the vaccinations to prevent deaths from the diseases.

We need to thank the good Lord and universe everyday for our good health and keep it maintained. The enlightened and wise soul asks and gives permission for their healing **ANGELS** to come and heal the body at night. This is like a preventive measure to ensure that we stay healthy.

GOD LOVES us and provides us the right foods such as fruits, vegetables, spices and the animals to provide us the meat we need to keep the body healthy. We are to give thanks for the food that is providing us nourishment. Also since I determined my health before I was born, I am not concerned when the medical world says certain foods and or drinks cause disease or are carcinogenic. If that was the case I would have been sick a long time ago. And even when people do avoid the bad foods and eat only healthy foods and exercise daily they still keel over from heart attacks and strokes. Of course, they do--it's their karma, not the food.

2.7 Using Energy to Heal Pain

As I have stated before, one of my earth missions is to heal others and I utilize it in my job as a certified nurse aide. (*Read why I was denied me my RN degree two weeks before graduation on page 71*). I take care of adult patients of which some have chronic pain that receive around the clock (ATC) pain medications. ATC therapy means that every four to six hours a patient receives a constant level of pain medication to keep their pain from reaching an intolerable level. ATC pain therapy is more effective than PRN (as needed) pain medication dosing, because patients may not ask for pain medications when their pain is at tolerable level. Instead they wait till the pain is at an intolerable level that when a medication is given, it will take longer to bring the pain under control or the patient ends up being given more than the prescribed dose. Three of the most common myths about pain medication I heard from patients during my nursing clinicals and at my job is: (1) they might become addicted (2) they can handle the pain and don't need those drugs (3) they did not want to be a bother to the nurses because they're busy.

The commonly used ATC medications are hydrocodone with acetaminophen (Tylenol) with trade names such as Norco, Vicodin, and Lortab. The others used are Neurontin, Dilaudid, and morphine. These medications are also used for breakthrough pain. Breakthrough pain is pain that occurs between set dosing. However, these medications are toxic to the body over time, especially acetaminophen. According to the Tylenol Professional Websites professional product information, http://www.tylenolprofessional.com/assets/TYL_PPI.pdf, page 11, "*Liver warning: This product contains acetaminophen. Severe liver damage may occur if: Adult takes more than 4000 mg in 24 hours, which is the maximum daily amount*".

So what health institutions do to prevent going over the maximum 24 hour Tylenol dosage is to integrate the regimen with morphine, dilaudid and/or Neurontin. Thing is when a person is taking these medications day after day, year after year, they eventually affect the liver, heart and other vital organs. That is why I am a big advocate on complementary alternative therapies (CAT) such as aroma therapy with essential oils which helps nausea and vomiting, medical acupuncture and hypnotherapy, Quantum touch, Reiki, and massage.

Some of these CAT's work on the gate theory of pain. In a nutshell the gate theory is that when the body feels different types of pain it is transmitted through particular pain receptors to the brain. In order to stop that pain we touch another part of the body by pinching or rubbing it which then transmits through other pain receptors to the brain. The theory is that the brain can only process one type of incoming pain at a time, and will shut off the oldest pain or touch sensation receptors in order to process the newest one. That is why when a child gets a scrap and mom then kisses the child's hand or rubs their back the child stops crying. The kiss and rub is the new sensation that needs processing and shuts off the old sensation. For example, when I have bumped my elbow funny bone I will start lightly pinching the opposite arm which stops the funny bone pain. Thus when using CAT's, instead of pain medication, it not only stops the pain, it is less toxic to the body.

Healing others is a calling and the person will be drawn to the correct healing method for them. True healers believe and accept that the energies can be channeled from **GOD**, their healing **ANGELS**, and the universe through them to others. Even though my healing ability is natural, I may still in the future take the Reiki or Healing Touch training.

The person called to healing heals without regard to who the person is. I have no prejudices, bigotry, hate, negative ego and feelings towards those who need healing. I do not do half hearted attempts in healing, it is all or nothing. I know that what I am doing is **GOD'S** work and praise and thank him for allowing me to be his instrument of healing. I never assume that I create the healing power--it is from **GOD**, the healing **ANGELS** and the universe.

Pain is energy and I feel that energy when I run my hand up and down a person's spine. Sometimes when I approach a person, I sense where the energy is emitting and I will touch it directly and the person is amazed that I went right to the area. Unlike Reiki and Quantum Touch healing where the hands are over the area, I lay my hand(s) directly on the area that the person says where it hurts and I direct my channeled energies to that area of the body. I have never been told by any person that I could not touch them. My hands do become warm from the energy coming through. I also heal using various shades of color such as yellow, purple, gold, red, green, blue and violent. What happens is that the color energy is first going into the area until I feel that the area is filled with the energy. Then I draw out the pain at the end and disperse it. For migraine headaches I will place both my hands on opposite sides of the head, direct the energy in and push the pain out the top of the head. Depending how long the person needs the energy is something I can also sense.

Thing about my healing energy is that it works even if the person has no idea I am sending it to them. For example, when I am holding a patient up on the side while a nurse is performing a procedure that is causing the patient discomfort or they say it hurts, I am directing my energy into the person. Sure enough, in a couple of minutes the patient stops complaining. I have also applied my energy on people who have had painful cysts and ganglions but I always tell the person, that my goal is stop the pain and they need to go to the doctor.

I also heal from distances by closing my eyes and imaging the person in front of me. I will place my hands on the part of the body that needs healing and send the energy. If the person has a disease such as cancer that is in different areas, than I take my hands and move them up and down the person's body. I also am **PRAYING** for the person to be healed when I am at a distance from them.

GOD only sends those to me who are accepting of receiving

healing energy, and I have not encountered anyone who has scoffed or made negative comments about my being a fake, or doing the work of the devil, or not having a degree or not being a doctor, or telling me that I should stop. The reasons are that I am much protected, as it is my earth's mission to help others.

Chapter 3 EGO AND PRIDE

3.1 Time to Let Go of Ego and Pride

Earth is a challenging place to live where we can either let our egos rule us and make us self center tenants instead of happy, positive and thankful tenants. Everyone has problems and or issues, some worse or more cumbersome than others caused by our egos. Ego and pride cause strife, wars and pain, can be as large as Texas, as arrogant as a strutting rooster guarding the hen house, or autocratic and despotic. It is what kills millions, manes the body, mind and soul. It is what affects our outlook on life and controls us. It causes us to be narrow minded, short sighted and intolerant of those around us.

That is why we get hurt and angry, have knee jerk reactions, seek out revenge upon others, gossip and bad mouth others, steal, lie, cheat, and refuse to take responsibility for our thoughts, actions, and deeds with rationalization. Ego limits us from understanding ourselves and expanding our minds and is self destructive and serves to hinder our **SPIRITUAL** growth. We all have allowed ego to rule our lives at one time or another as no one is immune from it. We also have our different levels of moral compass that will prevent us from acting out our ego based anger and rage. Bottom line; negative egos serve no purpose in an enlightened world.

When we let go of negative ego we find that we are happier and no longer sweat the small stuff. Instead of finding people irritating we begin to open up to listening and understanding others. We no longer feel threatened by what others say or how they treat us. Our lives become calmer as we no longer allow an ego based run away imagination that makes us think people are being offensive, out to get us or have ulterior motives.

It is hard for people to let go of ego and a difficult thing to say I am sorry and walk away. Our negative ego will not let us do that. We have to be right, we have to be on top, we have to prove we are better and then we have to prove, prove, and prove some more. And at the end of the day has anything changed? Have we won? Do we feel better? The answer is no and in all likelihood, we feel worse.

Ego is what kills **LOVE** in relationships. When people have unhealthy personality issues such as narcissism, selfishness, neediness, need to control, anger, cheating, lying, conning, and indifference then any relationship they get into is doomed to fail. We all have either been hurt by those types of people or have known someone who has been. The best way to avoid those types is to learn and know what **LOVE** really is and eliminate the negative ego from the thought process. Then you will attract the right person to you. When you practice what is healthy and right, then you know what is wrong in **LOVE**.

3.2 Arguing with the Family and Judging Others

Ego and pride are what causes the divided splits and riffs in families. What arguing family members refuse to accept is that they are all on the same level of arrogance, pride and ego which is causing the problem. When we partake in any squabble or fight, we are all allowing our ego and pride to rule the day.

Love means just walking away when the fight is going nowhere & you know you're not going to win.

The most common example is the sibling rivalry between people where one person is always intentionally saying or doing something offensive or hurtful to the other. Then the other sibling becomes mad and then they have to lash back at the other sibling. Of course, it leads to more negative comments, actions and arguing that keeps going on for years and no one wins.

For the person who finds them self arguing constantly with their siblings, parents, other family members and or friends, they need to stop and let go of the ego. No one wins and everyone always loses. We all have the power to let go of our negative ego. We will never change those around us; we can only change how we think and respond. We are not responsible for the other person's antagonistic behavior, but we are responsible for how we respond to it.

This means instead of having knee jerk reactions, we are to stop and surround ourselves and that family member in a golden light of **LOVE**. We are to let self **LOVE** flow through us as we say "I am sorry and I **LOVE** you" silently to the family member. Saying the **PRAYER** below over and over will elicit a sense of calm and **PEACE** within the mind. However, if the other person is out of control, one may have to extract themselves from the situation.

"My dear GOD, fill me with LOVE for (name of family member) and take this anger way now. Bring PEACE to my mind now. I LOVE you and thank you God. Amen".

Doing the above may be hard at first because of our egos but if we keep **PRAYING** and sending out that **LOVE**, it will turn the tide. As time goes on we may find that what that family member says will not cause us to feel as upset because we will have **PEACE** within our heart. Of course, our change of attitude will baffle that family member. After all, we have dropped the tennis racket and walked off the court and are no longer returning the other person's serves. Eventually, the antagonistic family member will leave us alone and go find someone else to argue with. This is because they need to make people feel as miserable as they are due to their insecure and angry egos. We may even find ourselves being less interested in going to every family gathering.

Prideful and cruel egos are taught to children by their ignorant and close minded caretakers whom lack the **LOVING SPIRITUAL** insight that is needed to raise an enlightened child. This happens when the child is exposed to the caregiver's criticism, intolerance, and attitude of superiority of others inside and outside the family. For example, a parent(s) who engrains into a child they are God's chosen disciple whose mission and duty is to convert all the sinners to be Christians. Or the parent(s) are members of hate groups and or religious cults that teach their children that it is okay to burn abortion centers, destroy property or even kill. **GOD**, our **ANGELS** and the universe want us as parents and caretakers to guide and teach the child to be **LOVING** people.

GOD is in control and creates only perfect souls, but it is our ego that makes the soul imperfect and ugly. Our ego creates the illusion that we think we are in control and the more we try to control everything in our life, the more out of control and uglier people become. Some of those illusions are:

1. Family and friends rebuke us, disappoint us, and they don't live up to our expectations.
2. Coworkers are sloppy in their work, can't get anything right, are constantly taking too long for breaks, have ulterior motives, are brown nosers and are not as good as we are.
3. Our kids seem to be lazy all the time, they never listen and do as they are told, they talk back, they sneak out of the house at night, and they lie to us.
4. Our spouses seem to be indifferent, uninterested, crabby, and argumentative.

If we continue to let ego rule our life then we will not achieve **PEACE** and **HAPPINESS**. For ego is reactive, it does not center the mind upon **LOVE** and understanding, but the negative.

I don't have to brown nose like those idiots to get ahead !

The first step to any type of healing is letting go of the negative ego. When we do, we can began to receive messages of inspiration from **GOD**, our **ANGELS** and guides which is instrumental in our healing.

Be free of ego based worry and anger by asking **GOD** to take it away, saying we are sorry for our past behaviors, ask for forgiveness and saying *"I LOVE myself as I am perfect in GODS eyes and so is everyone else"*.

If we let go of trying to control everything and allow **GOD** to take over, then surprisingly problems begin to resolve with less drama. However, the ego can be a strong adversary and that is why we **PRAY** to **GOD** for help.

"Dear Lord, I ask you to fill my heart with LOVE and understanding for those around me. Help me to guide others, and to be strong against the need to control, dictate and judge others harshly. Help me to know the difference between what I can take care of and what I cannot. I LOVE you and thank my dear Lord. Amen".

3.3 Guilt of Receiving Gifts

Guilt is a natural feeling from when we do something wrong and shows we have a sense of moral compass and a healthy ego. The guilt we feel when we receive a gift or present from someone is ego questioning our self-worth and **LOVE**. This guilt is a program that was implanted into our head, during a vulnerable time by those who did not have self **LOVE** and did not feel worthy to receive gifts themselves. Their unworthiness **MANIFESTED** into jealousy when they saw us receiving a gift and they became angry. We may have heard statements such as "you don't deserve to receive that", "you did not earn it", "take it back because the giver will expect something in return". And if we rebuked, the unworthy one may have crushed us further with threats or abuse.

Myself, when I was in my pleaser stage of life, I had no problem buying and giving gifts to people. However, I felt guilty and undeserving when I was given a gift which stemmed from childhood. Every time I had some candy or a toy my sisters would start pestering me to share the items. Of course, I would say no and they would tell my dad. Then my dad would take the item from me and give it to my sisters. Of course, I would start crying which resulted in my being sent to my room as punishment for being a selfish and ungrateful kid. What I learned was how to sneak around and lie to avoid sharing. I also had to prove I was worthy enough to receive gifts at Christmas and on my birthdays. If someone gave me something just for the sake of giving, my dad would call the person to make sure that I had not stolen or pestered the person for the item.

Here is the thing, children should not have to prove they deserved birthday and Christmas presents. The wise parent will set goals that the child has to accomplish everyday instead of just doing extra in order to get birthday and Christmas presents. If a child wants an extra toy or other item outside of Christmas, their birthday, or working hard to earn all A's on a report card, find a way for them to earn the money. For example when my son was 12 years old he wanted a $60.00 radio controlled car and asked me to buy it for him. I told him he could have it as a present for his upcoming birthday, but he said he did not want to wait. I suggested he take his manual push lawn mower and go earn money mowing lawns. Within three days he had the money but was short the sales tax so I paid that. He also took care of that toy very well because he had worked for it.

As part of our **SPIRITUAL** growth and evolvement, the universe will keep placing us into situations until we let go of the guilt of receiving gifts and presents. When I was married, my ex in laws would buy my husband and me expensive gifts such as TV's, furniture, beautiful jewelry, fine china, and silver plated flatware at Christmas time and for my birthday. I felt so guilty and had a hard time saying thank you. It took at least two years before I realized that yes I was worthy of receiving gifts and the guilt began to subside and saying thank you was no longer a problem. Then as the years went on the gifts became less expensive and smaller, and I did not feel slighted or disappointed that we were no longer receiving large and expensive gifts.

The following **PRAYER** will help absolve the guilt we carry about receiving gifts from people:

"My dear Lord, I give you my guilt for I am worthy and deserving of what you are giving me through others. Let me thank you for your blessings bestowed upon me and grant me HAPPINESS in knowing you LOVE and care for me. Thank you and I LOVE you my dear Lord, Amen".

We are all worthy of all the gifts, that **GOD**, our **ANGELS** and the universe sends our way. He **LOVES** and deems us worthy to receive not only his gifts and blessings of **LOVE** and compassion but the beautiful materialistic gifts bestowed upon us from **LOVED** ones and friends.

3.4 Patience and Compassion

I saw a bumper sticker that read, "I am not in a hurry in your universe, so pass me". We have heard that "patience is golden" but the flip side is "impatience is ego driven". Most of the world is in a big hurry to go somewhere nowhere fast. In that quest to get there we sometimes lack patience; but if we are impatient and rude and just cannot wait to get where we are going at the expense of others the universe will put plenty of impatient situations in our universe as a way to teach us to be patient and slow down.

1. Are we able to sit and listen to others talk without interrupting and injecting our two cents worth?
2. Do we find that when we are with friends on the phone that we are really listening to what our friend is saying or are we talking at the same time?
3. Do we get bored and impatient when someone is talking about a situation in their life?
4. Do we hear what others are saying or are our minds off in fluff land?
5. Do we get impatient and upset when an elderly person is walking with a walker in front of us and we cannot get around them?
6. Do we find ourselves squeezing by with an impatient and snappy "excuse me?"
7. Do we find ourselves becoming enraged when we get behind a slow driver?
8. Do we find ourselves telling our siblings, spouses, and kids if we find they are not fast enough for us "what's the matter? Why are you so slow? You need to speed it up! For Christ sakes are you going to be all day?"

Maybe it is not the other person—it might be you.

Patience....

It only lasts so long, then you get mad & leave

Then are the people who are compassionate and helpful to others but are critical to family and relatives they deem not worthy of their help, time or money. Those supposed caring and compassionate people deem the family member or relative lazy because they collect welfare instead of working, or are always asking for money because they do not stay on a budget, or they are the family alcoholic or drug user, or they are a hypochondriac that uses illness to make people feel sorry for them, or to get disability benefits when they really don't need it, and or the lazy family member who collects free money to keep on going to school instead of getting a job to support the family.

And, of course, there are the excuses to rationalize why these so called caring and compassionate people distance themselves from those family members.

"They put themselves into their current situation and therefore they do not deserve any of my money or help". "I don't have the money, I don't have the time, and it is not my responsibility". What the unworthy family member's situation is doing to the caring and compassionate person is making them uncomfortable, fearful, and even angry. The discomfort is that they might be taken advantage of. The fear is subconscious in that they might end up out of work and broke themselves. The anger is saying "I am better than you and how dare you bother me for anything because you don't deserve it".

But in **GOD'S** eyes we are all the same. And when we are faced with a situation that causes us discomfort, it is **GOD'S** way of opening our eyes and teaching us a **SPIRITUAL** lesson. We are to let go of the ego that is causing the fear, anger and judgment of others. We are to send **LOVE** and **PRAY** that **GOD** fills that person with **ABUNDANCE** and **LOVE**. Or better yet, send an anonymous monetary gift or buy something for the person in need and mail it to them. It will make us feel better and help us to release the negative ego that is ruling the situation(s).

Remember, if we do fall upon hard times, we will receive exactly what we gave out to others. If we do not help because we rationalize ourselves out of it, then all those we know will rationalize too. Ask **GOD** to release any fears we harbor through **PRAYER**. Fear is a killer and does harm. It only hurts us and all those around us.

Let go the negative ego, and fear; **LOVE** is you; it is me; it is all.

Chapter 4: CHILDHOOD ABUSE

4.1 Understanding the Reasons

Abuse is the selfish will of another imposed upon the mind body and soul. Excuses will not stop the abuse until a person chooses to end it.

Before going on, I have not suffered sexual abuse, incest, or pedophilia and I do not write about it. The person who commits these behaviors needs professional counseling. I, though, am **PRAYING** that through **GOD** and his **ANGEL'S LOVE** those who have suffered at the hands of the abusive deviants will heal and have **PEACE** within their soul, body and mind. May the words I have written inspire all to a higher **SPIRITUAL** understanding of why childhood abuse occurs.

We will have many different sets of parents as we go through lifetimes. Some we will **LOVE** and others we will not bond with. That is not to say that we do not have compassion or understanding because **GOD** will provide other avenues for us to experience parental **LOVE** with other people. This may be through an in-law or a friend's parent or being a caretaker of an elderly person.

My parents and I have had several lifetimes together to help them **SPIRITUALLY** grow in **LOVE**. However, again in this lifetime they repeated most of the same negative abusive treatment towards me. Needless to say, this created much sadness, anger and near hate as a child towards them. Even though they did not follow through on their end of the deal, I am still responsible for my choice and I have learned from it. Because I own my part of and accept what happened during my childhood, I hold no grudge or anger towards my parents. As far as talking to them about what happen, as I discovered years ago, they are not interested in accepting responsibility for their part. My dad became enraged and my mother said "Oh that was ancient history; I don't even remember half of it". (*The wise soul knows when to shut up*).

The childhood abuse we suffer on earth is not an accident. This goes against the accepted medical and psychological belief system that the abuse a child suffered is not their fault. However, according to the universe, nothing is an accident and all is planned. On the other side during the planning process we give our permission to allow certain people to be a part of our current incarnation to pay their karmatic debt through us to learn their lessons. We do this with full knowledge of what they did to us from past lifetimes. We also understand that there is the risk that an abusive situation could reoccur again. This is due to the abusive person becoming so wrapped up in the negative energies of earth and not sticking with their part of the plan.

For many, it is a challenging concept to grasp that we would choose situations that we know can lead to being abused. The two common notions are "why would I chose that kind of lifestyle" or "my *LOVING GOD* would never allow innocent children to be born into a life of abuse and poverty". Well, GOD did not choose to put us in our current life situation; we made the choice.

Let us say that an *ENLIGHTENED SOUL* allows his/her abuser from another lifetime to be in position of power, such as a parent, to rectify their abuse. When the *ENLIGHTENED SOUL* is born and the abuse is repeated, the *ENLIGHTENED SOUL* innately knows they are not responsible for the abusers actions and that the abuser is just creating more negative karma for themselves. The sad part is the child feels trapped and silently suffers in mental anguish and physical pain. Maybe the child will have the wherefore to *PRAY* for help.

Healing from abuse is what the victim needs now during this lifetime, so the victim does not become abusive and creates more negative karma. A person has to face and deal with the abuse in order to transformation into being a *LOVING*, happy and positive adult. Healing from abuse is possible and we can:

1. Heal the hurt, loneliness, desperation, self pity and empty void in ourselves and have a happy, *LOVING*, abundant and fulfilling life.
2. Stop feeling sorry for ourselves and blaming others for everything and take responsibility for who we are today.
3. Stop attracting dysfunctional people into our life.
4. Stop being abusive to others, and forgive those who have abused us.
5. Learn, know and understand what *LOVING* us is.

6. Have health, wealth, **LOVE** and what we deserve.

When a person goes the traditional counseling route, it can end up costing thousands of dollars. Counseling sessions usually last an hour once a week and can last for months to several years. Most insurance plans cover maybe 20 sessions a year. And many therapists suggest the client attend support groups and read suggested books.

I went through six months of counseling with my second husband thinking it would help him stop his drinking and be a better parent. At the time, I was a control freak and took no responsibility for my part of the problems. I was under the assumption that it was all my ex-husbands fault. It was like placing a bandage on a gaping wound. The behavior modification techniques only lasted for about two months and then my ex slowly went back to his old self and refused to go to any support groups. I just found myself becoming more frustrated until finally I had a dream where I was told by a guide to let go of control and trust God. I eventually left the marriage.

Unfortunately, my husband ended up married to another alcoholic who managed to manipulate him into spending all his retirement. Also during that marriage the ex racked up several DUI's and ended up in jail. With no money and in jail the wife packed up everything and ran off. When my ex got out of jail I took him in for about two months until he was able to get a place of his own. Sometimes we have to put aside our past differences to help others.

The other component of healing is **GOD** and our **ANGELS** are available to listen to us anytime and they do not charge exorbitant fees. They are the counselors and support group all rolled up into one. However, healing is not an overnight quickie fix but is an ongoing process of faith, **PRAYER** and affirmations.

Just like the good memories we have, the bad memories of an abusive childhood will never go away and cause lifelong problems if no healing action is taken. The person also runs the risk of marrying or living with an abusive person because that is what they are comfortable with. The following are some of the lifelong problems that we can carry into adulthood:

1. **Post traumatic stress syndrome (PTSS):** Childhood abuse is a daily battle to keep sane and in some cases alive. PTSS tends to occur when a survivor leaves the abusive environment to live on their own. Living and sleeping alone with ones thoughts and dreams is when PTSS usually rears its ugly head. Depending upon the severity, PTSS may require going to the doctor for medication and receiving traditional psychotherapy.

2. **Fear of abandonment issues**: This is due to the inconsistent *LOVE* a survivor received as a child and it created mistrust. The survivor was pushed away and ignored because their parents were cold and indifferent and it scared the survivor. The survivor felt emotionally abandoned because their feelings were never validated. The survivor was afraid to speak their mind because the parents would either ignore them more or they feared more abuse would occur. This is one reason why survivors became controlling and clingy partners in their relationships.

3. **Unresolved anger and hate**: The survivor was not taken seriously and or laughed at and or scorned for trying to be noticed. They were punished harder if they rebuked being hit or yelled at. They felt like chattel and used and not respected. The survivor is still upset because their abusers will not acknowledge their part in the abuse.

4. **Physical problems with the digestive system** such as heartburn, stomach ulcers, and indigestion, problems. This is brought on all of the above items.

We have to take responsibility and ownership of what has resulted from our experience and work at transforming the damages of abuse into *LOVE* in order to grow *SPIRITUALLY*. This means that if we turned into an abusive person, we have to stop it today and rectify the abusive behavior while we are still here. It is not too late.

According to the universe when we take responsibility for our part in our incarnation, forgive our abuser(s), be it parents, step parents or whoever, and heal we have stopped the abuse cycle. We are free to move on to a higher *SPIRITUAL* level on the other side and no longer have to be a part of that soul group. We are no longer responsible for them or owe them anything more on earth; it is up to us if we wish to help our abusers further.

When abusive people do not acknowledge and accept their part of the responsibility, they may play on the survivor's feelings by saying or doing things to elicit guilt in them. The survivor may hear that they are abandoning the abusers(s); or the survivor is a selfish human being that doesn't care about anyone but themselves; or the survivor may be cut out of the will, or the abuser(s) will try and get the rest of the family to turn against the survivor. This is because when the survivor leaves the situation, the abusers own fear of abandonment, desperation and defensive anger is rearing its ugly head.

Thing is, if the survivor is healed, they will not allow the guilt from the abuser(s) to bother them. Instead the survivor will be **PRAYING** for their abuser(s) instead of attacking back. Because of the ignorance of the abuser(s), they are creating more negative karma for themselves and by the victim choosing to walk away, this is fine with the universe.

During my healing from childhood abuse as an adult, my **ANGELS** channeled this to me: *"Your soul grows with LOVE in your heart. Follow the path that is a part of what you are and what you do, so you will lead the way with a light that fills the air with compassion"*. In other words, if we are sending out compassionate energies of *LOVE*, the abuser will not be able to avoid feeling it.

Once a person accepts and understands why they are responsible for what they chose in this lifetime, they can forgive those who have hurt them and stop the cycle. Then when the person is healed, they can stand in their own *LOVING* power.

4.2 SPIRITUAL Healing as the Adult Survivor

Healing from childhood abuse is complex and one should understand the universal and *SPIRITUAL* reasons why abuse occurs.

One of the outcomes of abuse are the throw away children living on the streets because of parents who are unable to provide and take care of their kids. Some of these children growing up on the street may be so mentally and physically damaged that no amount of counseling is going to help them. These children need our *PRAYERS* and financial help by donating to shelters that help get these children off the street. The same could be said for the organizations helping children living in dire poverty in third world countries in that they need our financial help. We all should be doing something no matter how small. Donate food, clothes, money and time. Every little bit helps.

Adult survivors, who are not healed, do not understand what unconditional and true romantic *LOVE* is and they commonly mistake the lust or jealousy they feel for their partner as true *LOVE*. The adult survivors emotional state towards their significant other and their children may *MANIFEST* as anger, impatience, insecurity, loneliness, fear of abandonment, and jealousy. When these unhealed survivors become parents they are unable to emotionally bond with the infant and or child because they did not experience maternal bonding or *LOVE* from their parents.

Ignoring the cries of an infant and children and not attending to their needs is engrained into the subconscious mind. It surfaces as frustration when the adult survivor is faced with caring for a crying infant or child who needs their constant attention. The cries trigger the adult survivor's subconscious memories of being ignored, neglected or beaten on when they were infants and or children. It brings out the buried scared feelings of mistrust, loneliness and abandonment. To cope with these raw hurtful emotions, the survivor rationalizes that "no came to help me so you do not deserve it either". In turn it causes anger and hence, the survivor lashes out by hitting, shaking, beating or sexually assaulting the infant and or child.

I remember when my baby sister would cry and I would tell my mom. She would say "let her cry, she will go back to sleep". This distressed me to a point of almost having an anxiety attack and I would sneak into the bedroom and rub her back through the crib slats to calm her. Sometimes she would fall asleep and other times she would keep crying. Then my mom would come into the bedroom and get mad and tell me to get out in a frustrated voice. Then she would have no choice but to take care of my sister. Then she would come out and tell me in an angry voice to stay out of my sister's room.

Adult survivors who as a child may have been deprived of basics such as clothing and adequate nutrition or doing fun things such as trick or treating (not due to religious beliefs), having birthday parties, spending the night at their friend's house, not being allowed to go school dances and etc. This, of course, caused sadness, anger and resentment towards the survivor's caretaker. This is why sometimes when the survivors child does anything fun, the survivors sad memories of being deprived surface and they become jealous of the fun the child is having. The survivor in turn becomes resentful and mad at the child and may forbid the child from doing the activity, or berate them into feeling guilty about the activity, or find a reason to punish or beat on the kid so they can't do the activity. If a person finds they are having feelings of jealousy and resentment, they should stop and assess why they are feeling that way. Take time out and say a **PRAYER** to release the anger or related negative feelings:

"My dear Lord, help me now to release these destructive feelings. I do not need them. Let your LOVE fill my being and give me understanding and patience in this situation. Thank you my dear Lord, I LOVE you. Amen".

Depending upon how needy, insecure and the severity the fear of abandonment is with survivor, depends how they react to their children's relationship with the other parent. The survivor may demand to have all of their significant others exclusive time and attention in order to fill the endless void of needing attention. The need for constant attention is like a drug which keeps the person from becoming anxiety ridden and nervous. This is why survivors become jealous and feel threatened when their significant others attention and time is directed away from the survivor to the children. The children then become a threat to the survivor's emotional state and significant others relationship. It can become a vicious cycle of abuse for the kids.

An example would be an emotionally needy alcoholic mother who is jealous and angry towards her daughters because they take attention away from her husband. She subconsciously wants to strike out at the daughters as punishment and so at the dinner table every night she tells her husband how bad the kids are. She knows this infuriates the husband and he ends up yelling at and whipping the kids with the belt and then sending them to their rooms. What this does is gives the mother a temporary feeling of validation and power, until the next time when the daughters make her fragile emotional state feel threatened.

For the adult survivor of abuse, ask **GOD** for the strength to heal and move on. It is important to understand and accept that what happened cannot be changed and that the survivor is not responsible for the abusers behavior towards us. **GOD** gives us the power to fill ourselves with **LOVE** in order to let go of anger and forgive the abuser and move on. Carrying anger, resentment or hate to the grave will keep the cycle going and will resurface in the next life time.

The following is the healing through writing and asking ARCHANGEL Michael to cut the karmatic cords of abuse. Use these writing steps as often as you need to as issues present themselves. This is also in the appendix.

1. Obtain paper and pen or pencil or sit at the computer keyboard and type it out.
2. Take three deep breaths and exhale as oxygen relaxes the body. Then ask **GOD** to place a white light of **LOVE** around your being. The reason for this is that when writing down the issues, emotions will be raw and the white light

of **LOVE** will help keep the mind on completing the exercise.

3. Write down or type out the issue(s) in as much detail as one feels they need to. After each issue, say it out loud and then say this **PRAYER**: *"My dear GOD, I am giving this (name of problem or fear) to you now. I do not need it and I am releasing it from my mind, heart and soul. It is no longer serving me to my highest and best good. I ask that you fill my being with your LOVE, forgiveness and understanding. I thank you for this lesson and those who taught it to me and now I am moving on. I LOVE you my dear GOD. Amen".*

4. After completion of the writing session, take the paper and tear it up and throw it into the trash.

5. The next step is to sit down and take three deep breaths and exhale. Then imagine surrounding the body with a white light of **GOD'S LOVE** and **PEACE**. Let the energy flow through the body and repeat the following: *"I am LOVED, I LOVE myself, I am worthy and deserving of*

LOVE and forgiveness of myself and my abuser(s)". Repeat this affirmation as many times as needed. The more this is said, the more the mind begins to believe it.

6. Next is to ask ARCHANGEL Michael to cut any remaining karmatic relationship cords with your abuser(s). This is done as you sit in a chair and imagine yourself in a room with your abuser(s) sitting across from you with a cord coming out of their heart to your heart. Place the abuser(s) in a white light of *LOVE* and ask ARCHANGEL Michael to enter the room and with his blue sword of light to cut the karmatic cords. Then *PRAY*: *"Dear ARCHANGEL Michael I ask you to cut any remaining karmatic cords with your sword of LOVING blue light. I am sorry that I have offended you (the person sitting across from you) and I release all attachments that created the negative karma with us. I command they be gone now! Thank you ARCHANGEL Michael, I LOVE you".*

7. Image seeing the cords fall to the ground and shrivel up into nothing. Tell the abuser(s) *"We are done, you are forgiven, thank you for the lessons, I LOVE you, you may leave now."* Image seeing them get up and leave the room through a door and the door shutting behind them. Then thank ARCHANGEL Michael and then leave the room through a door into a bright light of *LOVE*.

8. Also, we can ask ARCHANGEL Michael to help finalize and let go the negative memories by cutting the cords with his blue sword instead of wallowing in our misery which hinders us from moving on. Do this by sitting and visualizing that those negative memories have a cord attracted to us. Then *PRAY*: *"Dear ARCHANGEL Michael I ask you to cut these bad and negative memories with your sword of LOVING blue light to release these memories. I am sorry to those I have offended that created the negative memories and I command they be gone now! Thank you ARCHANGEL Michael, I LOVE you".* As the *PRAYER*, is being said imagine the cords dropping to the floor and shriveling up.

Another healing item that I wear is a purple disk from **www.purpleplates.com 1-860-830-9069**. This is a specially made metal fiber infused purple disk that works on the Tesla free energy principle. The theory is that the energy around the plates helps to accelerate the healing and thus return the injured area to its normal rate of vibration. A statement from an email I received from the company: "*We are a handful of mindful people working consciously to spread the Positive Energy of our products to the universe in the healthiest, most earth friendly way possible. In doing so, we are committed to producing our plates completely in the USA*". All I know is it works for me as I feel calm, **PEACEFUL** and energetic.

Also, people may chose face their abusers in person or write a letter to the abuser about what the abuser did, how the survivor feels, and why the abuser needs to apologize to the survivor. However, the survivor may receive a nasty and angry response, especially if the abuser is not healed. After all, the truth makes the abusers have to face the reality of who they are and take responsibility. But before doing anything ask **GOD** for protection by surrounding the body with a golden light of **LOVE** and saying the Tube of Light **PRAYER** that is in the appendix. This is so the abusers negative thoughts, actions and words can no longer affect the soul.

Unhealed abusers tend to deny their part and think that they have done nothing wrong. They will have countless rationales to throw back at their victim about how wrong the victim is and accuse the victim of lying; or that was ancient history and why are they bringing it up now and to forget about it; or how the victim was the one that caused the problems and how they are blowing things out of proportion and etc. To the abuser(s) denial and rationalizing is their coping mechanism.

Survivors may have to cut off relations with the abuser(s) even if it is the parents, siblings or other family members as we are under no obligation to continue to be a part of the abusers life. *Do not allow the abuser to affect you with guilt to rationalize how they feel*. As hard as it may be ask **GOD** and our **ANGELS** to fill that person with **LOVE**. Ask that the anger be released from our being to help us move on to the next level of our **SPIRITUAL** development.

Even with healing, there will be triggers and situations that will cause bad memories to pop up occasionally. Negative memories serve no purpose, so when a bad memory does present itself, **PRAYING** to **GOD** and our **ANGELS** can help stop the progression of the bad memory into a state of anger, sadness and despair. The following **PRAYER** can be said whenever a bad memory comes along:

"Dear GOD and my dear ANGELS, please take away this bad memory from me now. I do not need the memory; I am giving it to you now. Please fill my mind with your LOVE and PEACE. I LOVE and forgive myself, and thank you for taking the bad memory away. Amen".

4.3 The Creative Mind of Healing

In addition to the writing exercise, there are other methods that will help the healing process. Keeping busy in several areas are beneficial to ones physical and well being. One therapy is to utilize creative activities to keep the mind occupied. Photography, painting, ceramics, woodworking, writing stories, poems, cooking, knitting, sewing clothes, learning to play an instrument or singing can be a healing catharsis and creative release outlet for anger. Enrolling in classes to learn the above venues is also a good way to meet other people who share your passion.

When we are painting on a canvas the excitement and **HAPPINESS** from the creation we **MANIFEST** can release endorphins. All living creatures and inanimate objects have energy and when we are out in nature snapping photographs; nature's energy infuses into our minds, body and soul and creates a sense of **PEACE**. Later on when we are looking at the photographs, our minds are reliving the **PEACE** and beauty on that photograph and it soothes the anxiety. Myself, I find it relaxing and calming when I sit and edit the photographs I take. Woodworking, ceramics, sewing clothes, and knitting also can relax and stimulate joy and **HAPPINESS** from the beautiful objects we create.

Starting a regular exercising program is another avenue that helps heal the body. When a person exercises once a day doing aerobics, yoga, running, or brisk walking that gets the heart pumping, it release endorphins and help relieve anxiety. Also, if ones daily diet is made up of sugars and fats, i.e. fast foods, candy, and pop, the body's blood sugar level usually spite high and then falls drastically. This rise and fall is what makes us feel more sluggish and tired and the mind is not at its optimal functioning and can cause us to feel more depressed. A daily diet of healthier foods such as vegetables, fruits, grains and proteins helps keep the body's blood sugar at a constant level and thus we can function and think more clearly.

I find that when I use meditation, it releases endorphins through my body. I like to lie down on my bed instead of sitting on the ground with the legs crossed. Sometimes I will light incense and play new age healing music at the same time. The toning bowl website in the appendix has examples of new age music you can listen to. I also have crystals that I will place under my pillow during the meditation. What crystals do for me is they open the channels to my receiving answers from my **ANGELS** and guides. I also will put a crystal under my pillow when I go to bed if I need an answer to a question or dilemma. During a full moon I will not place a crystal under my pillow as there is too much conflicting energies and I have a hard time sleeping.

I then close my eyes and take about three evenly spaced out deep breaths and imagine energy entering with each breath. These are deep breaths that I feel expanding my lungs to their bases. (Breathing too many deep breaths close together too fast can cause hyperventilation). Then as I exhale I say to myself "I am **LOVE**". Of course, more deep breaths can be done if one feels the need to. I then clear my mind of all thoughts and then breath normally. I ask that **GOD**, my **ANGELS**, and **SPIRIT** guides fill my being with **PEACE** and **LOVE**. What I feel and experience may be different than someone else. I also have **INSPIRATIONAL THOUGHTS** that pop into my head. A person may also fall asleep and have a dream where they receive a message. I find this meditation exercise useful when I am having difficulty falling asleep.

Sometimes there are residue negative energies that are still in our living space that need to be cleared or cleaned out. For example, residue energies of a now ex-**LOVER** or spouse might be lingering in our mattress we shared with them. Or if they still are thinking of us those energies are sent to us. Or anything they touched we still have, their energies can still be permeated within it. Actually, when we hold on to items from past dysfunctional relationships we are done with, the universe views it as we still want to maintain a connection with that person.

Please do not do this exercise if you are allergic to sage

1. To clean or clear that energy from our living space is done by using sage wands. These can be bought at any new age bookstore. (Please do not use and set fire to the sage seasoning that is use in the dressing we stuff the Thanksgiving turkey with. (***It is not the same thing and not safe to burn***). When you light the wands, they will emit a fair amount of smoke.
2. Open a window to let out the energies that are being cleared. Clearing requires letting sage smoke into the entire living space, including closets and cabinets.
3. Waving the wand through cabinet space and closets is sufficient, and then shut the door afterwards.
4. For rooms, walk around once in a circle to allow the smoke to fill the area including the corners. It does not require filling the room with a dense fog of sage smoke to accomplish the goal.
5. As the sage smoke filters through each room, cabinet and closet, say *"If you are not of the light, you must leave. I bless this area with the LOVE and light of JESUS Christ. Amen"*.
6. When done, make sure to extinguish the sage and close the window. I usually dip the ends of the sage into a shallow level of water. Cleaning and blessing can be done on a regular basis as needed.

Writing creative stories and poems about our life experiences help us to reflect deeper on who we are and how our life experiences have contributed to who we are today. Also, one can use writing to channel in messages from our **ANGELS** for insight and guidance. Difference is instead of writing down the issues we have, we are asking for our **ANGEL's** messages.

1. Find a quiet area, and sit with paper, pen or pencil or type it out on the keyboard.
2. Take three deeps breaths for relaxation and to clear the mind. Then say the following **PRAYER**: *"My dear ANGELS, I am LOVINGLY asking that you bring to me your words of wisdom that will help me grow SPIRITUALLY through my writing. I am ready now to receive your words of LOVE. Please tell me your name after each message and let me know when the session is over. Thank you my blessed ANGELS"*.

3. When the messages come, they will be **SPIRITUAL** in nature and different from our ego based thoughts. The words may come fast, and if you cannot keep up ask your **ANGELS** kindly to please slow down.
4. At the end of the writing session, thank your **ANGELS** for their insight and wisdom.

When reading back the messages, some messages may resonate immediately, and other messages that do not, ask for clarification. Some of the messages I received years ago I did not understand, now make sense because of my **SPIRITUAL** growth. Since the **ANGELS** sometimes speak in an ancient context, I have had to update the messages to a modern context without changing the meaning for a clearer understanding.

The other aspect of healing is not to keep rehashing the past by retelling the stories over and over again once we let go of the situation. Retelling just keeps the emotional state raw and the universe looks at it as if we still want to maintain a connection. Sometimes, though, as I discovered, if we do keep talking about it, **GOD**, or our **ANGELS** or the universe will stop it.

One evening I was talking to a friend on the phone when the conversation drifted to my situation of being denied my nursing degree because of retaliation from reporting nursing instructor bullying to the colleges nursing department. My friend was asking how far I was going to go with the matter and I began to expound in great detail about what I had done and what I was going to do. As I talked I felt myself becoming angry and degrading the colleges nursing department and instructors. While in the middle of a long tirade, the phone went dead. When I was done blabbering on, I realized my friend was not there and called her back. She then posed the same question to me and I started to answer her with the anger still present in my mind and the phone went dead again and I called her back. She answered and said, "Okay, let's try this again". Then I realized that I had to stop.

"You know I think my **ANGELS** are trying to tell me to stop talking about the school thing. That is why the phone keeps going dead. Let's change the subject". I said. My friend agreed and once we did the phone quit going dead.

When you forgive and let it go, you do not keep talking about it. When I find myself doing it I say, **"Dear GOD take this memory away, I don't need it. Help me to forget about it. Thank you my dear Lord"**

Chapter 5: LETTING GO OF THE FEAR!

5.1 What FEAR is in Your Pocket?

Excuses are nothing more than our fears keeping us trapped.

ANGEL Quotes:
"If we do not face our fears and conquer them, the universe will keep placing us in situations until we do.

"To raise ones consciousness, one must release their fears. Fear is what hinders soul growth, and when the soul abates that fear, the soul then has the power to raise his or her consciousness. This in turn enlightens us to an understanding of LOVE.

"Fear will hurt, and it makes the mind, soul and body sick unless we let it go. When we take responsibility for our fears and ask GOD to take it from us as we do not need it; GOD will then be in control and we will be in our own power.

"Fear is nothing more than what was planted into your thought process at a vulnerable time in your life and causes problems throughout your life if not resolved".

Children are vulnerable to their caretaker's fears being programmed into them under the guise of **LOVE** and caring. Yes, we need protection from being hit by a car when crossing the street. We need to be taught to be aware of stranger danger. We need to be told no to going out by ourselves on a date at 13, or going to party at a friend's home where there are no adults. A caretaker(s) irrational and egotistic fears such as fear of abandonment, fear of losing control over their children, fear of loneliness, or fear of not having money usually leads to physical, verbal and psychological abuse.

In turn we can develop the same fears and repeat the abuse, anger and worry to those around us. We also fear looking within ourselves which can lead self medicating ourselves with drugs and alcohol to crush the pain.

We fear being alone so we become desperate and needy because we do not have trust in ourselves; only fear. The partner we choose in all likelihood is also desperate and needy and we stay because it is better than being alone. Being alone is scary because without the distraction of a partner, a person is left with facing their fears and an uncertain future. This is painful and thus we will do anything to avoid being alone. Thing is, this leads to one's life becoming out of control and hitting rock bottom.

The fear of not having, losing or spending money can cause needless worry or turn us into selfish and stingy people. We all have known people who despite high paying jobs or inheriting a lot of money are downright cheap. They have a fit if they have to part with their cash, or have a plethora of excuses to avoid spending their money for whatever. These are the people who leave the waiter or waitress a $2.00 tip when the bill is $65.00 or use a half off coupon at a buffet on a first date. Being cheap and selfish by holding on to money is a losing battle. The universe finds ways to pry open the cheapies wallet to resolve the fear of losing money. If the cheapie doesn't learn they usually pay the price before dying.

My ex-husband's narcissistic step father was so cheap that when my ex's mother became ill with a chronic disease, he feared losing all him money because of her illness. He locked her out their house when she was released from hospital, and cleaned out the bank accounts to hide the money from her. He divorced her thinking that it would protect his money but instead he was ordered to pay spousal support and she married another wonderful man. In his final years, the ex-father-in-law ended up in a nursing home dying and alone, as his kids had disowned him for what he did to my ex-mother in law.

To help be rid of the fear of losing money, using the first six steps of the healing writing exercise in the appendix can help. Sometimes a person may be where they cannot write and this **PRAYER** can be said instead: *"Dear GOD, please take away my irrational fear of losing money now from my mind and presence. I know that you will continue to provide for me and I give you this fear. Please fill me with your LOVE and PEACE to calm my fear. I thank you and LOVE you. Amen"*.

5.2 GOD Will Keep Us Following the Right Path

We all have a purpose on the earth to fulfill. Many children know from a young age what their life purpose is but are many times met with disapproval and discouragement by their caretakers. The caretaker's discouragement stems from ignorance, fear, the need to control, and what they think their child should do, or the caretaker lives their unfulfilled ambitions, dreams or life purpose through the child. Whatever the ego based reasoning or rationalization is; it is no match for **GODS** plan. The child will succeed, no matter what the caretaker's does to detour or prevent the child from their life purpose. Caretaker's need to let go of their egos, trust **GOD** and help guide the child on their destined path.

My situation is good example of why it fails for parents or other people to try and dictate what they think their children should do. I was born to be a photographer, writer and work in the medical field. At age six, I started pestering my parents for a camera every birthday and Christmas and the answer was always a no. Every time my dad brought out his Argus 35 mm film camera to take pictures I begged him to show me how to take photos. He would say that the camera was too complicated and I would never understand it and warned me to quit pestering him. In frustration, I began **PRAYING** to **JESUS** regularly to send me a camera and my **PRAYER** was answered four years later.

When I was 10 years old, during my grandparents annual two week visit out west, my grandfather had brought along his 126 Hawkeye Kodak camera. One day the camera it was sitting on the living room table and I began examining it keenly from all angles. My grandfather was sitting on the couch observing my intense interest and said I could pick up the camera and look at it. I picked it up and as I examined it, I told him that I had seen the same camera at the store and had wanted one since I was six years old. He replied, "Really, since six years old?" I nodded. Then out of the clear blue my grandpa asked, "Would you like to have that camera Missy?"

My heart began to race as my eyes widened with excitement. "Yes! Can I have it?" I replied back in a surprised tone of voice.

"Yes, you can. I think you will make good use of it", my grandfather said with a smile on his face.

Clutching the camera tight in my hands like a bar of precious gold, I ran through the dining and family room into my dad's workshop. "Dad, dad! Look what grandpa gave me!" I exclaimed loudly. "Grandpa said I could have his camera!" My dad stopped sanding his piece of wood, put it down and looked at me.

"Are you telling me the truth, Missy?" he asked in a disbelieving tone of voice.

"Yes!" I blurted out.

He then stared at me and said sternly, "You better be telling the truth or you're going to get a spanking". My elation trumped any fear from his threat as he quickly arose and walked out of the shop with me behind him to collaborate my statements with my Grandpa.

"Did you say Missy could have your camera?" my dad said sharply as he approached my grandpa.

"Yes, I did. It's okay. I think she will get good use of it. I know she has wanted a camera since the age of six and I want her to have it". My grandpa said with affirmation.

My dad stared down at me and then back at my grandma. "Did she pester you for it?"

"No she did not". My grandpa replied.

My dad looked back at me with a stern and disapproving look and said. "She can have it, but she has to share it with her other sisters. You understand that, correct?"

I nodded my head with an assured smile because I knew my sisters were not interested at all in photography or taking photos with a camera. I used that camera until when in eighth grade my parents bought me a Polaroid land camera.

As a kid I also spent hours writing stories and poems and wanted my parents to send them off to publishers and my parents told me, "No one is interested in your stories Missy, now drop the subject." I would also sit and sing my poems and my parents would shout from the other room, "Okay, Missy enough of your racket!"

I **LOVED** drawing Picasso type pencil artworks and one day showed one I drew of my grandma to my dad. Immediately, his face turned to a look of anger and I could feel the tense energy of rage he silently seethed at me. However, he said nothing. Later on that day when I got home from school and went to retrieve my paper and pencil, all my poems, stories and drawings were gone. I went and asked my mom what happened to my stuff while she was doing her housework.

"I don't know, maybe one of your sisters took it", came the curt and quick reply without her looking at me as she continued her work. After further inquiry, my sister Dianne who had stayed home sick from school divulged that "dad called today and told mom to throw away your stuff". I ran out to the dirty metal garbage can in the alleyway and when I lifted the dented metal lid, it was too late. It was trash day and I was met with an empty can. I was devastated and heartbroken, but never said a word because I knew my dad would use it as an excuse to punish me or worse yet whip me with his belt for bringing it up.

At age 12 I told my parents I wanted to be doctor and was told, "You can do anything you want". However, when I began high school I was told I was going to take the secretarial courses because secretaries make a good living and always have a job. Besides my dad's belief was that I would be getting married anyway and my husband would be responsible for taking care of me. So hence, I did not need college.

In my freshman year of high school I wanted to take photography, but my dad said "no, you're not going to waste my money taking photography, forget it". I was told to take home economics instead. I asked again in my sophomore year and the answer was still no. During my junior and senior years of high school, I was focused on finding a man to marry so I would be taken care of. However, that did not happen. When I graduated high school I went on at least 100 secretarial job interviews but never got a job.

After a two year period of personal upheaval, I finally married the second husband and got an underpaid job at an electronics plant. Then I landed my decent paying government job when I decided to take college photography courses which morphed into a part time business. Over the years I continued writing and finally landed a non paid position writing a photography column for a community newspaper, plus writing books and other venues.

As far as the medical field I had wanted to be an RN since the age of 19. I attempted several times during the course of 33 years to find a way to go to nursing school but roadblocks kept popping up. Finally at age 52 I was accepted into a two year RN college program. I passed the entire lecture portion with a B+ average and passed all the hospital clinicals until the last one, where I encountered instructor bullying. The instructor utilized profanity during post conferences at our group, lied to us, corrected and embarrassed me in front of patients and my classmates and she put me on a work plan because I refused to divulge sensitive information to her on other instructors. I reported the bullying to the schools nursing department.

As a result, the nursing department placed me into a second clinical with the intent of failing me as retaliation for whistle blowing on an instructor. The instructor I was assigned to, had passed me in a previous clinical, however, the second time around she bullied me and threatened to fail me every clinical day. I noted, though, she treated my clinical mates with respect, did teaching and was nice to them. At the fifth week she put me on a work plan and told me I had to be perfect, which she knew was an impossible goal. Sure enough two weeks before I was to graduate the program she said she was failing me because I was an unsafe and incompetent practitioner. However, I withdrew before she put the grade on my transcripts. I appealed up the administrative ladder but was told sorry, that is how our teachers teach and too bad if you did not like it. Two years of hard work down the drain.

Even though the nursing department thought they were retaliating, I know that this situation will be rectified as those arrogant and egotistical woman have no power over *GOD'S* plan of my completing any part of my life mission. All it shows is their ignorance and lack of understanding of how the universe works.

GOD and our *ANGELS* want us to be happy; they do not want us to be miserable. If we are not doing what our life purpose is, the universe and *GOD* will keep putting it in front of us causing a feeling of restlessness and anxiousness. It may be a hobby we spend all our spare time and money on. Or it could be as fleeting as singing karaoke in a bar once in awhile. When we experience passion and *HAPPINESS* for a part time activity we wish was a full time endeavor, this is because we know that is what we should be doing. If we do not follow the path we chose, we will be plagued with misery, sadness, anger, unfulfilled lives, illness and other negative emotions. But instead, we continue to get up on Monday morning to face the dread of going to a job that we hate and or feel unfulfilled at.

And, of course, we have the endless rationales' of why we are where we are at. "I need the money to pay the bills and put food on the table. I got a family to take care of. I don't have the time for it. It won't pay the bills. That costs money. I can't do that because (put in the reason). My husband or wife won't let me. I am too old for that now. My family never supported me doing that". Then again, we have been conditioned from knee high to a grass hopper by others who never achieved their life purpose that it is irresponsible to go chasing uncertain pipe dreams that may not pan out financially.

The majority of people who do not follow their life purpose have allowed the programmed thoughts of society, their parents, teachers, churches and other sources to dictate their life. We are expected to be productive citizens and work a job that makes the most money in order to live the good life. The good life is having a nice large home, new cars, fine clothes, nice vacations, sending our children to the best schools, being members of an exclusive and expensive country club, having status in the community and church and other expectations. This takes money and the way to get that money is to get an education in a field that pays good in order to fulfill society and family expectations. This does work for those whose life purpose is to do that, but for those who are suppose to be on a different path and ignore their calling, it will eventually fall apart.

For example, it may **MANIFEST** when a 50 year old successful attorney decides to become a **PEACE** Corps volunteer in Brazil. As a teenager he had done volunteer work and enjoyed it and wanted to get a degree in social work. However, being from a prestigious and wealthy family, he was programmed that he to follow in the footsteps of his forefathers to fulfill the family tradition. Reluctantly, the man did as he was told. However, by the age of 50, the man was at the end of his rope, frustrated and the urge was so strong to help others that the money, prestige and wealthy lifestyle lost all meaning and value. He gave it all up and fulfilled his life purpose and found his **HAPPINESS**.

Fear also keeps up from fulfilling a life purpose. The fear of failure, the fear of not making enough money to live on, the fear that we will be rejected by our family and peers, the fear that our spouse will leave us, the fear our kids will hate us; all real to us but not to **GOD**, our **ANGELS** and the universe. To be rid of the fear, it needs be replaced with faith. This faith is what reassures us that **GOD** will take care of us when we are on the right path and fulfilling our life's purpose.

To help materialize the occupation we want to do, visualize or role play we are working in it. Feel the great emotions and benefits that go with it. Write down how we will accomplish the goals of achieving that occupation. Believe and have faith and ask **GOD** to help make it a reality. The universe may **MANIFEST** small opportunities at first, which eventually will lead us to where we are suppose to be. Have an open mind and be ready to receive and implement what is sent our way. Remember too, that we did plan out how we were going to be taken care of financially and the universe will provide it to us. If we have doubts and fears about accomplishing our goals write them down. Go through each one and say the following **PRAYER** every time. Also say it when you feel any of those fears popping up in the future.

"My dear GOD and my ANGELS I am releasing and giving you all my doubts and fears from my soul, mind and body into your hands. I ask that you fill me with your LOVE, assurance, ABUNDANCE, and blessings. I ask for your guidance and to show me what I need to do. I ask this of you. I thank you and I LOVE you. Amen".

Chapter 6: DYSFUNCTIONAL LOVE

6.1 The Cause and Effect of Dysfunctional Love

Ah yes, dysfunctional **LOVE**. You want a **LOVING** relationship, but they never seem to work out. Well, **GOD** and the universe will not send us our true **LOVE** of our life if:

1. We are not mentally healthy in the arena of **LOVE**
2. If we do not understand what unconditional **LOVE** is
3. If we are still living in a state of dysfunctional **LOVE**

It is only when we make the choice to heal and have a healthy understanding of what love is, is when our true **LOVE** shows up--no matter how long it takes. The following are channeled words from the **ANGELS** on dysfunctional **LOVE**:

Love is...

Sharing the moment.

"*Our past is our learning ground. We all have to look at our past to know what we need to learn for the future. LOVE is omnipresent in all life, as we know it. It is what keeps us alive. Therefore, it is not a silly notion to assume that what we have experienced in the past is not carried with us throughout our future lives. Though, people will say that there are no past lives, this notion is farther from the truth than your travels throughout time. All that you know within your soul is your truth; you cannot deny it.*

"*We are to learn that LOVE is forever. Why must you people of earth repeat the same mistakes with the same people? Are* you that closed off to the presence of **GOD**? Why do you continue in a negative mindset of hate, mistrust, and indifference? There is so much more to **LOVE** than the narrow thoughts that you keep boxed within your brain. Why does the soul allow the temporary setting of the third dimensional world to dictate how they will treat the one they proclaim to **LOVE**? Even when you decided to interact with new souls, you repeat the same lessons.

"**GOD** is forgiving, and you can be too. We need not choose to return with the same souls or new ones, and think lust is **LOVE**. And at the beginning of the relationship you treat your partner well, but then fall back into your same pattern of destructive **LOVE**. Do you know that you will continue to return and repeat the same lessons until you learn what **LOVE** is instead of lust? Lust creates boredom; **LOVE** is lasting. Until you awaken to an enlightenment of understanding what **LOVE** is, your existence will be like a merry-go-round.

"**LOVE** is beyond conditions set by our experiences. **LOVE** is more than the limits set by our defenses that build a wall of protection from pain and hurt around us. LOVE is all encompassing, not the small perimeter we set within our minds. **LOVE** is endless, not finite. **LOVE** cannot be bought or sold as it is a given from the universe, with no conditions, no boundaries, and no limits. **LOVE** is a bright flame that illuminates the world, yet people douse the flame with fear, hate, insecurities and evil".

LOVE is a **GOD** given gift that people on earth have made into a complex emotional learning process that will run us through the gantlet of anxiety, sadness, devastation, mistrust, and broken hearts. And it does not help when we have an unrealistic and unhealthy expectation of what we think **LOVE** really is:

a. **LOVE** should be constant attention, romance and endless sexual excitement.
b. Never ending worship from our partner and being showered with gifts all the time.
c. Expecting our partner to be there only for us all the time, living up to our expectations and changing after we marry them.

d. Thinking that jealousy proves our partner **LOVES** us and we have right to control what our partner does.

However, by learning and understanding why people have dysfunctional issues with **LOVE**, we can heal and move forward to be the **LOVING** beings that we are suppose to be.

The root cause for dysfunctional **LOVE** is what we learned in childhood from the environment our caretakers provide us. If a child is in a household where they are exposed to alcoholism, drugs, constant abuse, ignored, and not shown **LOVE**, they become fearful and mistrusting children that grow into **LOVE** starved adults. These children are so desperate for a scrap of **LOVE** from anyone, that the child will go up and hug strangers in public. These children are so use to inconsistency that they cannot handle stability. That is why they think their friends who come from **LOVING** families are not normal. These are the children who act out nonstop for attention whose parent's beat them for being bad instead of taking the time to find out the reasons why the child is acting out. These are the children who will either abuse animals or **LOVE** them obsessively. They are children who grow up and marry the alcoholics, criminals and abusive significant others. These are the women we work with who tell you how bad their husbands treat them and then say "You know, though, he really is a good man".

From my first cognitive memories at three, my life seem to consist of being yelled at and whipped by my dad's hand on my behind for being a bad girl. At age six, I took the family kitten one day and swung it by the tail into the wall several times and then stepped on it until poop came out its rear end. Then I laid the kitten on the bed and kissed it. I did not feel that I was being mean to the kitten; I thought my treatment was normal and okay. When my dad found out about what I had done, I got a hard whipping which left me confused. Why did I get whipped, I was not being mean, I had not done anything wrong to the kitten. Needless to say, the abuse got worse as I got older and my confusion carried on into my school life, and I was always getting in trouble for acting out.

Regardless of whom the person is or what their station in life is all people need **LOVE**. Even the people that our egos tell us are not worthy of our **LOVE** such as murderers and rapists. If we hate those who we deem not worthy of our *LOVE*, we ourselves are just creating our own negative energy and we will have some reciprocal event happen to us to balance out the energy.

Of course, if a person is repulsed by the thought that they should even consider giving *LOVE* to those types; then the person is missing the point of what *LOVE* is about. Remember; *GOD LOVES* all his beings and if we cannot *LOVE* all of our fellow man, than why should *GOD LOVE* us? It is not our place to hate others, it will only eat us up inside. Replace hate with *LOVE* and let *GOD* do the rest.

The need for *LOVE* and to be *LOVED* is also a big money maker. Dating and matchmaker sites, (I knew a woman who paid one matchmaker site a $2000.00 membership fee), books, seminars on how to attract a man or woman, going to the $2.99 per minute sham psychics for *LOVE* advice, singles dances, clubs, fairs, cruises, trips and conventions, and marriage sites offering exotic foreign woman who want to be *LOVING*, good wives. You get the picture.

For example, I know men who have utilized the exotic foreign women marriage sites that did not work out for them. Once the women got over to the United States and became Americanized, they ended up divorcing their husbands. At my government job I worked with an Asian woman who had divorced a man six years after he had brought her over to the states, so she could marry another Asian man who was a U.S. citizen. Another man I know had his Asian Internet bride take off a year after she arrived in the states. Another man at work ended up filing bankruptcy because his foreign Internet bride was a drug addict and drained his bank accounts before she took off with another man.

For whatever ego driven reasons, people are spending their hard earned dollars in search of *LOVE*, and either their return on investment pays off or most of the time does not. However there is a better way to find the right person that saves the lonely hearts hard earned money. Trust *GOD*, the universe and our relationship *ANGELS* to bring us the right person.

Of course this requires letting go of the ego which is causing the reasons most people use the above resources: loneliness, insecurity, need to find a person they can control, neediness and or desperation. People will deny that they do not have those issues as there is nothing wrong with them. If there was nothing wrong then these people would not have a history of failed relationships. These people also tend to blame the failures on the other person instead of stopping the blame and *LOVING* who they are instead. If we do not *LOVE* ourselves; how can we *LOVE* others?

6.2 Trying to Change others doesn't Work

Susan: "*I use to have anxiety attacks whenever a boyfriend would be away from me over night or on an extended trip. I could not sleep, eat, and I would cry and have to talk on the phone for hours with anyone who would listen. I felt so lost and alone. I finally accepted that the men I had interacted with on this earth were never going to give me the LOVE I needed to have for myself. During my healing, I learned the reason for my irrational behavior was because I did not LOVE myself. I was depending upon every man who came into my life to fill my endless empty pit of neediness. When I took responsibility for my emotional state and asked GOD, and my ANGELS to heal me, my empty pit filled up with their healing love.*"

If a person has ulterior selfish motives, or are needy and desperate they will attract the same type of self centered and selfish person to them who will have a price on everything and not know the value of *LOVE*.

Tammy: "*I was engaged to a man who left me for another woman. His reasons for leaving me was I did not contribute to the household, I was not working what he considered a regular job, he was tired of paying for everything and claimed I was sexually dysfunctional. Two weeks after he married the woman I received a nasty and mean email from her stating that all I had wanted her now husband for was his money, never appreciated anything he did, and I was not a real woman. But she was because she would greet him at the door with LOVING arms, a hot meal on the table and a clean house. And everyone was laughing behind my back at me because I was crazy. And that if I did not stop stalking her husband she was going to put a restraining order against me. I was dismayed to read that it was the same reasons he given me for leaving and divorcing his first and second wife. I thought it was their fault and that I was different. It was my* *wake up call to how bad my neediness to keep a man at any cost had blinded me to who he really was and I vowed to heal myself with the Good Lords help."*

If our **LOVE** life is an endless stream of **LOVERS**, non commitment, the wrong person and relationships that never last or work out, it is due to the same dog and pony show program replaying on the same channel in our minds. It is easier and comfortable to stay on the same channel than exerting the effort and work to change the program. We figure it's not broken why fix it; because it's not our fault; it is the other persons fault. But it is broken because we do not **LOVE** ourselves enough to fix it.

The only way to change the program is not by changing others but by changing ourselves. We cannot change anyone unless that person wants to make a change. People have the illusion that once they are living with, engaged to or married that they can get their significant other to change. Or a person thinks they are different and special from all the other people their significant other has been with and they can fix their significant others dysfunctional relationship patterns. Well, it does not and will not work because we are just another player in their roulette game and will lose every time they spin the wheel.

6.3 Characteristics of Dysfunctional LOVE

*"I'm going to marry you" he said to her at the end of the first date. Then on the drive back to her house he started in, "Do you think I'm okay, do you think you could **LOVE** a great guy like me?" At the house, she got out of the car and ran for the door, went into the house and turned off the porch light. He never heard from her again, despite his calls and he could not understand why. "I am such a great catch who just wants to take care of that special someone".*

An abusive person is controlling, domineering, needy, and desperate tends to come on strong, pushy and charming. They are masters at being nice, kind, sweet and **LOVING** to hide their true selves but only until they gain control over the other person. Then the phony persona comes off and the mean, cruel and abusive behavior surfaces in order to force their partner to change into what the abuser thinks they should be.

The controlling person can show their true colors at the start. For example, on a first dinner date at a Chinese restaurant, the man I was with questioned my menu choice of food because he said he had eaten it before and did not like it. Then he tried to convince me to order what he liked because he knew I would like it better. Then the guy started endlessly questioning me about my past relationship history and private life. When I mentioned that my son was good at fixing things around the house, he jumped in and offered to do anything I needed done any time. Needless to say I recognized he was a control freak and since I had driven my own car, I got out of there as soon as possible and I never went out with him again.

The narcissist is charming, cares only about themselves and is incapable of *LOVING* another person. They chose partners who will worship them and do everything they want. A narcissist charms their partner into thinking that they appreciate their unique characteristics and differences, and pretends to accept the *LOVE* the other person bestows upon them. The narcissist only stays as long as the partner is of benefit to him or her. As soon as the other person wises up and stands up to the degrading treatment, the narcissist is out of there. Since the narcissist never was in *LOVE* with their partner, the partner is of no longer of use, nonexistent and the narcissist could care less what happens to them. A narcissist views all assets as theirs and will do everything in their power to take it all and avoid paying spousal support. If there are children, the narcissist may fight for custody to avoid paying child support. If not, they will rarely, if ever, come around again to see them. The narcissist will be hooked up with another vulnerable partner in no time because they need to be admired and worshipped.

A potential abusive and controlling partner will treat anyone he/she considers of a lower status then them with animosity, anger, disrespect, or a condescending attitude. This can include food servers, maids, store clerks or members of the opposite sex. Thing is, this eventually is how the abusive and controlling persons partner will be treated once the abusive and controlling person thinks they have control over them.

A partner who is constantly telling us any myriad of negative and degrading statements such as: how messed up we are, or how we need psychiatric help or we could not survive without them, it is not about us. It is because our partner is actually talking about whom they really are and how they feel.

The media and society as a whole reinforce dysfunctional **LOVE** as the status quo in many ways. Romance novels, for example, are unrealistic stories based on dysfunctional **LOVE** relationships of non-commitment, indifference and fear of intimacy. People spend millions of dollars every year buying these books. The typical buyer of these books tends to be a woman who needs to vicariously live through the drama of the commitment phobic, abusive male, or the female character who sacrifices their self worth to win their mates **LOVE**. If the reader of these romance novels develops a mindset thinking their **LOVE** life should be like the books they are reading, they will not be happy in a comfortable and **LOVING** relationship. *A real life loving relationship can and does become routine, comfortable and sometimes downright boring with occasional disagreements over all kinds of things*.

Another dysfunctional accepted society fueled mindset is that if we really **LOVE** someone, we are to stay and stand by that person no matter how bad the relationship is. Most organized religions teach that marriage is through thick and thin (sorry but there are limits), that divorce is wrong and couples should stay together for the children. Society, as a whole, lauds those who suffer almost to the point of martyrdom, when they stand by their man or woman to help them through their transgressions or suffering, i.e. the politician's wife who stands by her husband when he accused of fooling around with interns. This is not martyrdom, but a misguided mindset besieged with defensive rationales and future heartbreak. And besides, when a person catches a cheating partner, the cheater will make sure they don't get caught the next time around.

Bottom line: Wasting time on dysfunctional **LOVE** only results in feelings of anger, fear, abuse, heartbreak and worthlessness.

Here are a few truths about dysfunctional **LOVE**:

1. If a person has cheated on previous partners, they will do the same to new partners. It is only a matter of time. If our **LOVER** is cheating and lying on his significant other to be with us, he or she will do the same to us. Once a cheat and liar, always a cheat and liar.
2. We are no different from the countless other dysfunctional people that our partner had before us. We are just another number in his/her game of roulette and once the excitement is over and he or she is comfortable with us they will revert back to their real selves.
3. If a potential partner is a liar, sneaky, an alcoholic, druggie, thief, gambler, spendthrift, and selfish, before they met us, do not expect them to change for us.
4. If our partner is always making excuses or causing fights to avoid seeing us, they will never commit to us.
5. If we are expecting our partner to be more **LOVING**, it is not going to happen no matter what we say or do. Even if we leave, the partner might change for awhile, but will revert back to their true selves.
6. A partner can only put on charming façade until they think they have us where they want us.
7. Things that bother us before marriage do not get better but become worse.
8. If our partner is cheap in courtship, he/she becomes cheaper in marriage.
9. Once a victim, always a victim, until we stand up for ourselves.
10. If our partner's friends, money and obsessions come first--we will always be second.
11. Jealousy is not about **LOVE**--it is about insecurity and the jealousy will result in accusations, loss of privacy and abuse.

12. Ultimatums do not work--they only drive the other person away.

6.4 Desperation, Neediness and Obsession

Desperation is another ego based emotion that is the result of allowing ego based situations to get out of control by not learning the lessons we are here to learn to keep from becoming desperate.

There is desperation from a physiological need stand point i.e. Maslow's hierarchy of needs. A person may be hungry and homeless and feels desperate. So they steal food from a store, rob someone or burglarize a home to get money to survive and then they get caught. The person either ends up convicted and in jail or maybe they get counseling and help. What leads to that point of desperation? Was it alcoholism, drugs, mismanagement of money and losing everything? Whatever the reason, it means our egos were ruling us instead of trusting **GOD** to help us learn the lessons needed to prevent from becoming desperate.

Desperation also creates the neediness and obsession in dysfunctional romantic relationships. We find ourselves living in constant fear that we might lose our significant other. The following are the two common signs that we have lost all sense of who we are:

1. We fear losing our significant other, so we become pleasers in order to keep our significant other in our life. We become clinging vines, jealous, mistrustful, and abusive. It leads to anxiety, and feelings of abandonment. The other person in all likelihood is a taker and drains us physically, mentally, and financially.
2. We give away our money to and sacrifice our time and energy on the other person. We will give up everything; including our kids to keep our object of obsession. This ego based emotion has the consequences of causing physical and psychological illness.

Obsessional **LOVE** is a condition that may not rear its ugly head until we end up in a relationship that triggers it. I discovered it was a problem I had no idea existed until after I had ended an obsessive relationship. By the end of the first day when the reality hit me of what I did I began going through withdraws. I was having constant anxiety attacks, I had no appetite, I could not sleep, I could not stop obsessing about him, and I cried constantly. After a week I finally went to the doctor to obtain medication to calm myself.

When the medication made me feel stoned and melted all my troubles away, I realized that was how people become dependent on prescription pills. So I quit taking them and in my desperation I asked **GOD** for help. The next day I received six books in the mail from a friend on healing from obsessive **LOVE**. I learned that my obsessional **LOVE** was a culmination of my abusive and **UNLOVING** childhood upbringing that I allowed to continue into my adult life. It was an ah ha moment and time to let go of the negative and destructive ego that was causing my dysfunctional **LOVE**.

6.5 Take a SPIRITUAL Healing Journey with God

I began my healing by **PRAYING** and asking **GOD**, to take the neediness and desperation away and filling me with self **LOVE** of myself. My healing was a lengthy process with some backsliding, but I kept up my **PRAYING**. Here is a **PRAYER** that I wrote down and said often.

"Dear GOD, my ANGELS and universe I need your help. I ask that you take away from me this ego based desperation and neediness that is causing me pain and sorrow. I ask that you fill my heart; mind and soul with your LOVE of understanding and grace. Please be with me and lead me to those resources and people who can help me overcome this. I also ask that you help me to recognize the dysfunctional situation(s) for what they are in order for me to heal. I ask this of you my dear Lord GOD. Thank you and I LOVE you. Amen".

Remember that **PRAYERS** do not have to long, just a heartfelt cry or thanks from the heart. Healing in order to have self **LOVE** takes work and is an ongoing process. The goal of **SPIRITUAL HEALING** is to bring **LOVE** and **PEACE** within soul, mind and body.

1. Understand that a person's desperation and neediness is an ingrained thought process that needs intervention from **GOD**. It may be at a point in our life that is almost like an addiction where one has to have a man or woman in their

life at all times or they will suffer anxiety attracts, cry, and feel lonely, empty and worthless. To rid ourselves of these dysfunctional emotional responses, we have to take responsibility, turn off the current program and let *GOD* take control.

2. No matter how much it hurts, we have to let go of grabbing on to the wrong people. We have to let go of any relationship that is destructive, even if means being alone.

3. We will find ourselves thinking of old comfortable memories which can be a challenge to be rid of because they have been engrained for so long. This *PRAYER* will help to stop them in their tracks:
   "My dear GOD, take this memory away now. I no longer need it as it does not serve me to my highest and best good. Thank you. I LOVE you. Amen". Repeat this as much as needed. It will take time, but after awhile the memory does not come back as often. And when the memory does, the emotional aspect such as anger or extreme sadness will be greatly lessened or even gone.

If we are alone for the first time in our life in order to heal, we may suffer anxiety attacks because of the subconscious program of the fear of abandonment. This is common and again we have to *PRAY* to *GOD* to help us.

"Dear GOD, be with me now and take this fear away. I LOVE you, I LOVE and forgive myself, and the fear is now gone. Thank you. Amen". Repeat this over and over until the feeling of PEACE is within your being.

If one feels the need to read self help books, ask *GOD* to help find the best one that suites your situation. Not all self help books are the same.

Another aspect of being alone and dealing with the anxiety and loneliness is that we may find ourselves wanting to talk to or call family members and friends several times a day. Yes, they do care about our recovery, but this will wear very quickly on them and they will start avoiding us. Our friends and family have their own lives and do not have endless hours to sit and talk on the phone or in person. However, *GOD*, our *ANGELS* and guides are the ones who are listening and they never tire of us talking a blue streak to them. So, when one feels the urge to make that 10th call to a family member or friend, stop and **PRAY**:

"Dear GOD, please give me the strength to overcome this anxiety. Do not let me burden my family and friends with this anxiety. Please take it away now. I LOVE you and thank you. Amen".

Again, say this **PRAYER** over and over until you feel the anxiety dispersing away. Now, if we really desperately need to talk to someone, this is the time to find a support group and a sponsor that is willing to take calls. And, of course, keep **PRAYING** the above **PRAYER**.

A common mistake men and women make is using their young children as a surrogate partner to fill their empty void or as our sounding board. This is a selfish thought process as young children are not mature enough to handle the parent's emotional upheaval. Also, by treating a child as a surrogate partner, the child will take over the role of the other parent. This causes problems when the adult begins to date other people because the child will view the other person as an intruder and a threat. And, as the child grows into an adult, if the parent does marry, the child or children will make sure that their mom or dad is protected from the new wife taking their inheritance when she or he dies. It is a never ending battle.

Sally: When I started dating John, he had invited me to his house on the fifth date for dinner and to meet his 11 year old daughter, Sydney, who he had custody of. As soon as I arrived I noted she was like a subservient little wife, setting the table, interrupting any conversation I was having with John telling him that she cooked everything special just for daddy and endlessly needing daddy's help. When I offered to help get the meal served, she said "no thanks, my daddy and I will take care of it". At the dinner table she made John's plate saying my "daddy likes the way I do it". After dinner she rushed around to get the dishes loaded into the dishwasher. When John and I went into the living room to sit and talk on the couch, Sydney came in with a cup of coffee and cake, sat it on the table and then sat down next to John and gave him a big hug and said, "I LOVE you daddy, see the cake I brought you!" Of course, John hugged her back and gave her a kiss on the forehead and said "thanks honey". Then he asked if I wanted some cake and then got up to go get it with Sydney right behind him. Afterwards we started to watch a movie and no sooner than when John sat down, Sydney was right on his lap with her arms around him throughout the movie never moving from her spot. I felt like the third wheel. After the movie when John walked me out to my car, Sydney was in tow hanging on to her daddy's hand. I said my thank you and good evening nicely, left and never went out with John again. I was not interested in being the second wife.

The following are other additional healing things I found helpful during my healing period:

1. **Journaling**: Whenever I had problems sleeping and or eating from the anxiety, I wrote my issues in detail, how it evolved and the trigger that caused the obsession. I allowed myself to feel the anger and hurt that went with the situation. Then I reflected on each item saying this *PRAYER*: *"My dear GOD, I am asking you LOVINGLY to please take this anger and hurt from my being now. I am giving it to you to keep. I am free of this emotional baggage that has caused me to not LOVE myself and others in a healthy way. I ask that you fill my mind, soul and body with your everlasting LOVE now. Thank you my dear GOD, I LOVE you and Amen"*. This *PRAY* helped transmute my negative emotions.

2. **Past life readings**: This was helpful in gaining enlightenment to what lifetime the neediness and desperation had started in to work on my issues. I would not recommend utilizing the gypsies' or the $2.99 minute phone psychics. The gypsies will lure you in with a reading for like $39.99, and then they end up telling you it is going to cost anywhere from $200.00 to $3000.00 for them to get rid of the spell or curse. They will have you do ridiculous things like putting hard boiled eggs in jars filled with water or writing a word like fear three times on a piece of paper and burning it. (No I did not go to one). The $2.99 phone psychics are shams so I utilized legitimate psychics at an established bookstore called Vision Quest in Scottsdale, AZ. Website information is in the appendix.

3. **Crystal toning bowl sound therapy**: A friend of mine had musically tuned crystal toning bowls that helped clear my chakras of any remaining blockages. Crystal toning bowls are musically toned to the different body chakras. The sound they emit is similar to when a person wets their finger and runs it around the thin rim of a 24K lead crystal glass, except the sound is a 1000 times more magnified with the toning bowls. More info at the web site in appendix.

4. **Listening to new age healing music during writing and meditations**.

I found healing from obsessive *LOVE* tends to take a shorter time than recovering from grief. It took about six months to get over the initial emotional turmoil. Obsessive *LOVE* is more like a drug in our body, when we don't have it we suffer withdrawal symptoms similar to like when we stop a drug. Once we get the obsessional *LOVE* out of our being we no longer have the withdrawal symptoms. Grief from the loss of a *LOVED* one takes much longer to heal and sometimes people die from a broken heart due to grief. My experience with the feelings from obsessive *LOVE* and grief was different. During the obsessional love withdrawal, the adrenaline was going nonstop for at least a month and I lost weight and could not sleep. With grief, I felt like I had an elephant sitting on my chest and was in a depression for at least three months.

Of course, I still had more healing to go through and lessons in learning to let go when a relationship was not working. But I never again fell apart emotionally like I did because of spiritual healing through *GOD*, my *ANGELS* and the universal energies of love and *PEACE*.

Remember: When our healing is complete and our being is **LOVE**; that is when we are ready for our true **BELOVED** to come into our life.

6.6 Bringing in the LOVE We Deserve

If we are following our road map of what we think we want in *LOVE* and keep getting lost; it is time to ask *GOD* for directions and follow his path that will lead us to the right person.

We need a spark to start a fire, and if there isn't a spark when we meet someone and date them, there is not going to be fire of LOVE. In other words our inner voice tells us if we are going to fall in **LOVE** with that person we meet. We will know it either when we first meet the person, after the first date or soon thereafter. If we think that if we hang around with a person long enough we will eventually fall in **LOVE** with them, it is not going to happen. Either we are in **LOVE** with someone or we are not. If we are hanging on to someone because we think we owe them something, or don't want to be alone or don't want to start over again, but are not in **LOVE** with them; the relationship will not last. When another person comes along we do fall in **LOVE** with, we will leave the other person for them or vice versa. It is best to move on and let *GOD*, our *ANGELS* and the universe lead us to true *LOVE* instead of hurting the other person or us getting hurt.

ANGEL Quotes: *"LOVE is the redeeming feature of our souls on earth. We must believe in ourselves to allow the LOVE of the universe to expand within us and to others, for that is all we will have. Remember who you are and why you have chosen your current incarnation. Your ANGELS are here to help you. Ask and you shall receive".*

"Sing forth with a voice of determination. Let flow all words of knowledge. LOVE is what we need to live and is the lifeblood of our souls. Keep free the flow of LOVE to and from the heart, and our lives will be blessed by GOD. For his commandment of LOVE thyself, must be lived so we will be able to LOVE our neighbor. LOVE is to be practiced within the context of giving without expecting a reward. It is better to reward yourself with the knowledge of knowing that you have given LOVE to others and yourself. LOVE is the way".

First and foremost we need to trust *GOD*, our *ANGELS* and guides to take over and be our matchmakers instead of us doing the same old methods that have not been working. We then need to release our ego driven beliefs and emotions through *PRAYER*.

"Dear GOD, my ANGELS and guides, I ask of you to help me find my BELOVED who is meant for me. I also ask that you help me to release any doubts, fears, anxieties, neediness and desperation that will keep me from

your guidance. I also ask that you fill my heart
LOVE and help me to forgive all those who have
'D me, and who have hurt me throughout my life.
. sorry to all those who I have hurt and caused
pain. I ask this my dear Lord with LOVE and thanks.
Amen".

The **PRAYER** below is for whenever one feels overwhelmed with anxiety, frustration, neediness, desperation, loneliness, anger, and sadness related to not having a loved one around.

"*Dear Lord, help me now to overcome this (negative feeling) and take it away, I do not want it. I am replacing this (negative feeling) with your LOVE as I know that my beloved will come when I am healed and ready. I LOVE and thank you. Amen*".

At night, before falling asleep we can **PRAY** to **GOD** and our **ANGELS** to continue to heal any remaining negative ego emotions within ourselves. Also, if we are having a problem with **LOVE** in a relationship, ask your **ANGELS** for an answer in the dream state. We may have a vibrant and interactive dream, especially if a full moon is out, or if we are very tired or exhausted we may not remember the dream. Dreams are best remembered when we get regular, uninterrupted sleep several nights in a row.

Love is sharing quality time together.

When we tell the universe what we want in a partner, state the positive qualities this way: My dear Lord, what I am choosing in my beloved is that he/she is nice, kind, loving, has self love for his/herself, is a good and wise steward of their finances, etc. Do not state what you do not want. For example: My dear Lord, I do not want to deal again with another narcissist like I had before. I also do not want another needy guy/girl. When we state that we do not want something, we are reinforcing that we still have a problem with that issue(s) and the universe may send us through another lesson to work it out.

Remember **SPIRITUAL HEALING** is not a quick overnight fix as it takes dedication and focus. It is a lifelong process that never ends because if we stop it; that is when the sneaky ego waltz's back in with painful engrained memories of the past. If a painful memory does pop up, this **PRAYER** can help squash it: *"My dear GOD, I asked you to take this memory away now. I do not need it. I LOVE you and thank you. Amen"*.

No matter what the situation is or how the person is treating you, **LOVE** is what heals. Always proclaim "I **LOVE** you". No matter the time, no matter where you are walking, living or working; center your being in the present and say within yourself **"I LOVE you"**.

ANGEL Quote*: To be alone is a time to heal. It gives you time to think, to gather your thoughts, to ponder. To let go of ego is to release control. You heal your mind, body and soul with self **LOVE** of thyself. When you **LOVE** yourself, you can **LOVE** others.*

If we allow our hearts to be filled with past relationship bitterness and hate instead of **LOVE**, it turns us non-trusting, miserable and non-**LOVING** people. We might think it will not, but the bitterness will surface and **MANIFEST** in one form or other. Be it in our face, body, health, and attitude or thought process. Most of the time, I can feel the bitterness from a person in my presence; but I had two different incidents where I was caught off guard. The two men, whose hateful and angry vibes directed at me, caused me to break out crying. The reasons for their anger were minor, but since these men had serious personality issues, they blew the reasons out of proportion.

One man was an ex-boyfriend's ex-father in law who had survived the horrors of being a Jew in Nazi occupied Europe and the other was a Vietnam vet with mental issues I worked with at my government job. Personally, I think if there had not been other people around they would have physically assaulted me. For this hard lesson, I learn to protect myself with the following **PRAYER**. This is from a **PRAYER** booklet that a friend gave me back in 1996 called the Heart, Hand and Head Decrees PRAYER booklet by Elizabeth Clair Prophet. Even though I have read news articles written about how Prophet was a cult leader, I do not feel this **PRAYER** is cultish and I say it all the time because it works for me.

BELOVED I AM Presence bright,
Round me seal your Tube of Light
From Ascended Master flame
Called forth now in **GOD's** own name.
Let it keep my temple free
From all discord sent to me.
I AM calling forth Violet Fire
To blaze and transmute all desire,
Keeping on in Freedom's name
Till **I AM** one with the Violet Flame.

6.7 Keeping the Flow of LOVE Going

The ANGEL Mennose offers an insight of why **LOVE** is vital to our lives. *"**LOVE** is the redeeming feature of our souls on earth. We must believe in ourselves to allow the **LOVE** of the universe to expand within us and to others, for that is all we will have".*

The ANGEL Jonas: *"What you say is what it will be. You must direct where your thoughts of **LOVE** go. Hail that we receive blessings when we have a new understanding of what we need do to survive the strife. We can perish under a weight of indifference foregoing within even a heart of gold. Forget what not is yours. It was, it is, and it will be. Release and understand. No man stands alone, nor is he to blame another. All our souls are entwined within the universe. When our actions are done karma misses no one. There is payment to be made for the atonement of the soul. Sin is only what you* *think it is. All is lessons, nothing more. But we cannot do our lessons with reckless abandon, as for the earth has and it is reaping the sorrows of karma."*

When a person understands the healing power of **LOVE** and accepts it for what it can do for them, they make changes in their life. These changes are to keep the flow of **LOVE** flowing out to others. A few examples of those changes: The person may start saying have a blessed and **LOVING** day at the end of their phone voice message. Telling people more often **GODS LOVE** is with them. Repeating "I **LOVE** you" when walking out amongst crowds in a public area or when driving. **PRAYING** more often that **GOD** blesses all they know with his **LOVE** and **ABUNDANCE**.

On my business cards I have the line "**LOVE** creates miracles, let it flow". On the back I have a tip chart with the heading, "*Tip right—GOD will bless you for your generosity*".

The following statements are reminders to keep **LOVE** at the center of our lives.

1. If we go with the flow of **GOD'S LOVE** and stop trying to control, and let go of the same old memories we keep thinking of in our mind every day that keeps us from achieving, our dreams will come true.
2. *"Let go of the ego as it limits our life. Let the divine be our inspiration and allow the miracles to happen. When we are faced with a problem, it may not be our fault, but it is our responsibility to heal it by saying **I am sorry, please forgive me, thank you and I LOVE you to the divine"**.*(From Hawaiian healing system: http://www.self-i-dentity-through-hooponopono.com/contact.htm).
3. When we show our **LOVE** for ourselves and others through honestly and diligence in our work and life we are walking the path of success.
4. When we always say "I **LOVE** you" and freely give it; it brings you back to **GOD**.
5. Creativity is **GOD'S** way of saying that we have the ability to think in the moment and thank the universe for the prosperity we have.

Always thank **GOD** for everything. Live in the moment, reflect on what is perfect at the time and thank **GOD** for:

- The roof over your head
- Having food to eat
- A car that is running and getting you to your job
- A healthy body, mind and soul, a healthy family and pets
- The people who care and **LOVE** us
- The job that is providing us with money to buy what we need to live on and enjoy life with

Aren't you glad that GOD, and the ANGELS never say, "That's not my job!"

96

Chapter 7: THE ANGELS WORDS OF LOVE

7.1 The ANGELS

An opening message from the ANGEL Theresa:

We travel not lightly in the realms of this world, as we needlessly carry a burden of uncertainty.

We should allow ourselves to let go of such needful things. Like the gold of the land, the jewelry of the mind that only decorates and adorns the fringes of the truth. Our lives are more than what we think them to be.

Like a new born kitten that is limited by its' self contained world; we have used our eternal free will to slot ourselves into a disbelief and cynicism of doubt, and lack of faith.

To cover and decorate the truth with the babbles of nothing, that concedes not through time from our grasp. We allow these babbles to weigh down our souls of light.

*Listen to what you say. Are your words of **LOVE** and truth or do you speak the words of negativity?*

*No more can the earth hold what you spew upon its dirt. No matter how you justify those words and deeds, you need not lose your birthright as the souls of **GOD** because of it.*

*Letting all your power flow and harming not others with your negative passion, shall transcend the many vibrations of **PEACE** and **LOVE**. You know of those souls who carry sadness. They know not how to release, the darkness that permeates their entire being. It will drift over to you. Therefore, you are to **PRAY** to us **ANGELS** for that souls blessing of enlightenment of **LOVE**.*

And you are to surround that person, in the violet glow of light. It shall transmute their sins that befall what the sadness may recall. Lose not that hope and let go their pain; for they are lost, because they have chosen that path.

*Your **PRAYERS** of hope and **LOVE** are like the white dove of **PEACE**. It shall bring the light of **PEACE** to calm the soul of its sorrow and misery.*

It takes an open mind to listen and be willing to receive the messages and words of **LOVE** from our **ANGELS**. Life is

LOVE and *LOVE* is what heals and makes the world a better place to live in.

We all have our guardian *ANGELS* that are with us from birth to our death. I went to a Doreen Virtue workshop back in 1999 and she led us through an exercise to hear our angel's names. The only two names that came through were Hanna and Morna. (Incidentally, the four hour workshop only cost $40.00 and she was still doing angel readings afterwards).The *ANGEL* messages and verses written in this book were channeled back in 2003.

The steps for channeling your *ANGEL'S* messages can be found in the appendix.

Each *ANGEL* has a unique personality and different way of speaking. I have listed **The ARCHANGELS** who are Omni present and will help with learning and certain strengths. This information can also be found at any number of ANGEL Internet sites.

Auriel: Light of *GOD*. This *ANGEL* will help us with discovering our future, our life's purpose and accomplishing those goals.

Gabriel: Man of *GOD*. Relays information to us about *GOD'S* plans and our life's purpose and will also send the help us need to complete our life's mission.

Haniel: Mercy of *GOD*. In charge of beauty, *LOVE*, HAPPINESS, pleasure and harmony.

Michael: *GODS* right hand man. Fights evil and challenges those with evil or negative intentions. Expands our thinking capacity and gives us courage for *SPIRITUAL* experiences.

Raphael: *GOD* has overcome. Works with artists and healers to help them recognize and bring forth their creative abilities.

Raziel: Secret of *GOD*. ARCHANGEL of Mysteries who provides the inspiration to find the truths we seek on our *SPIRITUAL* journeys.

Uriel: Fire of *GOD*. The ARCHANGEL of prophesies who will provide us with the flow of new thoughts and ideas to help us complete our goals and life missions.

7.2 Words for Reflection

GOD'S LOVE is perfect and all he has created is perfect. Our *LOVE* for mankind should be perfect. But life interferes and we put our barriers up that hinder that free flow of *LOVE*. We make unconditional *LOVE* more complicated than the perfection it is and find it hard to let it flow.

1. **PEACE** is a cherished time of reserve that our soul needs to refresh oneself.
2. **Quiet** is the motion of nothing and nothing is sometimes what the brain needs.
3. **Release** is letting go of the soul's sewage that plugs up our *SPIRITUAL* growth and development.
4. **Listening** to our heart for what our *ANGELS* are telling us. Following their message is wisdom; thinking with ego instead is less than foolhardy.
5. **Looking** only with egotistical eye limits our *SPIRITUAL* growth. Seeing and knowing the truth with our *SPIRITUAL* eye is life changing.
6. **To bless ourselves** with the white light of Christ shall free our soul from anger, hate, distrust, and the other negative emotions.
7. **We are to free ourselves** from the rigors of negativity, for it will hurt our soul in the end.
8. **To move forward** in life is not to dwell on what should have been but to live in the presence of *GOD'S LOVE*.
9. **GOD is there** in all we are, so we are to be his beacons of *SPIRITUAL LOVE* to our fellow mankind.
10. **Keep all LOVE** within who we are; for we are to think and live in *LOVE*.
11. **The GOD voice** of the universe is all for the world to know. We cannot let ourselves go on through our earth life without understanding that the *GOD* force of *LOVE* is keeping our souls free.
12. *Casting* the pearls of wisdom out amongst the unenlightened is foolhardy and can result in a negative backlash.
13. *We cannot force* anything upon anyone or ourselves. If we do, we are striping others and ourselves of *GODS* divine plan intended for us.

7.3 The ANGELS Life Guide for Earth Survival

We hear what you say; we will come when you call and will bring you our messages of love, hope and inspiration. Be ready to listen and learn as we have the knowledge and fore thought to see that the people of earth need us to help. We can heal if you ask. If only the lands of the earth would open

What cat's guardian angels see.

*to the universal concepts of **LOVE** and **PEACE**. Then there would be no such thing as karma. As karma stands it is only what we keep living, it not need be. Release those bonds of restrictions; you know that you are a part of life and an intricate part of the universal plan. Your soul is endless, **LOVE** thyself, and be not of sadness and understand those who know not. You will know what your life is when you open up to us and allow us to speak to you. **PEACE** is with you.*

*People live in a fantasy world of what they think **LOVE** is. Yet, they deny the reality of what they know. Free yourself from the restrictions of negative actions by asking us **ANGELS** to help. We are the messengers of **GOD** and we are with you. Yet, you understand not that concept for you value not the relationship of **ANGELS** for your well-being. We are here and we **LOVE** you, so be of good mind to seek our guidance. We lead you not, but lend a hand. We care and **LOVE** you, but not intrude. Hear our voices, and listen to their words, for you need the **LOVE** to learn, understand and in turn give the **LOVE** you have to yourself and others.*

*We must not allow ourselves to die a death of uncertainty. Our souls are a result of what we have learned and **MANIFESTED**. We are where we are to be at this point in earth time. It is as we speak the tongues of ages, a wisdom that bestows our being. Remember who you are and it is **GOD'S LOVE** that matters and is important in the development of your soul. We are not to allow the negative perception of others, as they pass through our life, to affect us. Those negative souls tend not to conceive of a life outside their **MANIFESTED** box of isolation. It is like the boundaries of the druids, which keep them surrounded in uncertainty. What you are meant to see is the fields of life, of **LOVE** and the freely given knowledge that keeps the mind aware of the endless universal flow of energies.*

The blessings of the heavens are bestowed upon you. To which you value what you have, what you know, and how you utilize all that is within your grasp. Yet, many wander within their unproductive abyss not knowing that it is more than it can be as they still have not yet found the key.

*Let go of what you need not and allow the faith of **GOD** to lead you. You are as whom you are; learn that what is to be. For life is at hand for you. For we are never alone as we travel on in the universal realm of **LOVE** and its being.*

*The strength comes from our **PRAYERS**, faith, and a belief in **GOD**. **GOD** is **LOVE** and can help us. Our **ANGELS** and guides are there to channel the answers of hope, **PEACE**, and the meaning of **LOVE** to us. We are to live our life as **LOVING** beings and not implementers or sufferers of abuse. Take the reins of life and let your heart lead the way.*

*Embrace the light of **LOVE** for you are one with **GOD**. He has you in his sight. You are never alone and will never be without. Be right in the midst of life and **LOVE**. Forgive those who have trampled you for they will come to you for answers as you become blessed with the knowledge of ages. Praise **GOD**.*

Behold a beacon of light that shall light your path so the rotting darkness is no longer destructive. All in due time will the justice of the earth be foretold, when all who seek to relieve that presence of hate, anger and abandonment will be vindicated.

*It is not fair that you hurt within. Trust the spoken words from us, your **ANGELS**. Find ye the comfort in knowing we are here, we leave not the trail which is the path on which you follow.*

*Keep on the path where you find the truth. Learn and remember that truth is laid out by those souls who have traveled before you. Things change not; only if you choose to do it yourself. Fear not the unknown; it is only your ego playing tricks. Let not that negative ego influence you. Your heart knows best. We know all what is there for you, you need only to sit quiet and listen. Nothing is forever except **LOVE** and we are to cry forth with passion of **LOVE** in our hearts. It fills the void of hate and the deep pit of despair. If you leave behind all those imperfections and travel forth with us **ANGELS** showing the way, you shall see the rewards of greatness.*

Live for the now, dwell not on the past. To live in the past will gain you nothing and your life will stay unaccomplished. Forthwith, only then will the earth be free, when life is met with the cries of men shouting, "I release the past, it is the freedom we seek and need!"

*We chose our life here for whatever lessons we need to learn. The past is only necessary to clarify a lesson in comparison for what the present relates to. Relive not the dramas of the past. Bring forth the truth of light. We all have the knowledge to light the flame of truth, **LOVE**, understanding, and the need to let go of evil.*

*Evil around you is like the shell of a walnut, and the **LOVE** of us **ANGELS** is like the translucent mist that encompasses all within your space. The soul without the light of **LOVE** that allows evil to set up the barriers of a walnut shell will not have the strength to crack the shell open. For the barrier keeps your **ANGELS** at bay, for we are not allowed in. Yet, we **LOVE** and **PRAY** for you, that the small flame of knowledge will expand and burn away the shell of evil with an explosion of **LOVE**.*

*Life is to understand who we are and that **LOVE** encompasses those around us. We **ANGELS** leave not our senses and always travel on the path of **LOVE** to which all is invited. Your soul will know not **SPIRITUAL HAPPINESS** until* *the light and flame of one's understanding of LOVE is lit for all to see.*

What you may think is your thoughts are what we are saying. We know because we see. Though many souls chose not to listen to what we say. Even if you have not the gift of sight through your third eye, so be it. It may not be of your choosing. But, you can MANIFEST those same ideals of LOVE and understanding of one's self so the illumination of the flame is glowing within your soul.

LOVE is a bright flame in a room of darkness. Even if you are in the midst of the darkness, does the light need to go out? No. The candle is like the body. It knows the flame will burn because the wax is like the LOVE of our souls, it feeds the flame, and the light will burn.

The flame of LOVE may attract all, but if the evil of another soul comes close, the flame will burn them like the wings of an insect that has too close to a flame. The person of knowledge and knowing can only be in that space with the flame, and instead of being burned, feels the warmth of the other souls LOVE.

The mind is the core our bodies. It is within the brain that the mind knows and expands to which our bodies react. If you should not rest from the disturbances of your surroundings, or do not surround your SPIRIT with the white GOD light of PEACE, LOVE and protection, then your body will MANIFEST the evil which bombards you and which hinders your SPIRIT within the realm of its life force. The life force of LOVE protects us so we need not suffer what negativities are around us. Believe in yourself and what GOD has for you, and you shall be free of the illnesses of the soul, which are greed, hate, anger, indifference, intolerance, selfishness, insolence, and destruction. Live free in the SPIRIT of LOVE for LOVE shall be free within you.

You are to let go of the attachments for they hinder your growth. You need not what languishes in your midst because what you think is real is not. LOVE is the only real thing that is needed to release your past. Care not for the physical and tangible assets that you behold, for they are temporary, you are not. When you let go of all burdens that make you not whole, you will not feel the need to grasp for more. Only when *you feel the light of **LOVE** from your heart, will you live the life you are meant to have.*

*So you say 'I cannot let go, it is not easy. I cannot burn the bridges; I must hang on to the things of my past!' Listen to what you say, for it is your ego speaking, not your heart. When you put your trust into the divine you will know the truth to release, you will find yourself letting go of all what you think you should keep. **PRAY** for the strength to let go of those negative emotions. The emotional bond of mistrust and anger is what keeps the door shut, and keeps the divine from opening it to **LOVE**.*

***LOVE** is the key to letting go of anger, hate, mistrust and deceit. Flush the mind of the sewage of the lower vibrations of life. We are not to live in the past of sorrow, but we are to learn and move on. It is a lesson to know how to let go. Be free and let the truth be a part of thee. Care not that others think you are callous for disposing of what you no longer need, because they too may be in the same boat someday. Understand yourself and know you are to be free to **LOVE** again. It is the sadness that shall pass with what you call time. However, to the universe no time shall pass until you forgive and release. Your time is now, not later and all is perfect in its place for you.*

*I Morna, **ANGEL** of **LOVE** and understanding, know that it hurts me to view the people of earth crying over **LOVE** that hurts, **LOVE** that is destructive, and **LOVE** that has gone awry. It is of both genders that create the havoc that lets not their soul grow in the understanding of **LOVE** for others and within their souls. It should be of good knowing that they the ones who hurt, can lift the blinders of ignorance. We the **ANGELS** can be of assistance to opening that knowledge of what you need to know from your past so you can begin to rectify the present.*

*Your life will be entwined within the realms of **LOVE**. We are the souls of light to which we have traveled throughout the universe. To allow our hearts to know of the past is to rectify the problems that occur in the present. This being the core truth of the **LOVE** to which we are entitled to upon the planet earth. For all those souls who we have known and will know, that we gave negative **LOVE** to, that when we met again, free* *of negative emotions, our lives will then be fulfilled and balanced within the universal realm.*

*We cannot allow the negative emotions to interfere with our growth. We must allow ourselves to learn what we need to know to experience and understand we need the light of **LOVE** to guide us to the realms of understanding of what beholds your place in the core being of life. Many souls heed not the words of the Lord, the masters, and their **ANGELS** and thus they carry on with the mistakes and anger within their souls.*

*Let not the hindrances of the earth keep you from finding true unconditional **LOVE**. Listen to your heart and those who have gone before you who can share their knowledge and **HAPPINESS**. We are humans who are to be happy in **LOVE**. Our lives are not to repeat the same transgressions with the same people to where it shall be a continuance of damage to the soul. Life is about **LOVE** and our **LOVE** is about others. We are to learn and live in **LOVE** and thus bring forth a light of understanding to which is what our lives are about. The light of **LOVE** is with all of us. We are to know the warmth of that **LOVE** and experience it to the fullest.*

Your free will in a relationship can be like playing with fire around a dry bush. You can do as you wish with the fire of desire, but if you set it upon the dry bush, which is void of that desire, the bush will burn hot and then burn out. Then your soul is left with nothing but the karma of that intrusion.

From Mary:

*Letting go and releasing negativity, be it fear, pride, or ego is needed for understanding a life of **LOVE**. Our minds can be complex, or simple in their thoughts; too over focused or scattered amongst the universe.*

*We are beings who need to **LOVE** and accept what others are. We cannot constrain another's life, within our narrow frame. We are free to choose and endure the pain, or the pleasure of what we deem sane.*

However, the mind shall never be caught within the bounds of life, because our souls are of a brighter light.

The heavens open up their gates and let all knowledge be fate, to which we take and make our own.

*Our choices are many, the realms not too few. And that endless cycle of **LOVE** is due when all the earth sings in harmony.*

Cast off the shadows of doubt, they strangle out the life; your light of holiness shall shine, when in one you are, divine.

*Let not yourself hinder on within a false sense of wrong. Only know that all is right, within the soul of your might. You stand the ground and feel the strength of **GOD** and fate.*

*Us **ANGELS** and all the saints have set the path to make a way for those who seek all truth and past debate. Never once is the soul to doubt that life is here and now.*

*We live our life to which we need, but not a life of greed. If we steal from the **ENLIGHTENED SOULS**, they understand the karma of what will not be the thief's to keep.*

Remember we are who we are and our life is only but one step of many in the universal trail of light.

From Jason:

*Carry forth the torch of patience, a bright white light of **LOVE**.*

So many others will see the way that leads to righteousness.

Yourself within knows all that is now; blessed be the root of karma that teaches the lessons of life and all that it tells.

From Morna:

*The one simple thought that binds a magnificent heart. Our minds flow freely with thoughts of **LOVE**.*

*We are to toss thoughts of insecurity away into the dark abyss, from the place where the **LOVING** minds of souls occupy.*

*When we call forth those who know to live a life of **LOVE**; nevermore will the flame die, when the entire world joins in passionate **PEACE**.*

*Cry forth a song of **LOVE** let all who hear know; Thou are to understand that **GOD** is here. He cares for all the earth, with simple words of passion, deciding vows of **LOVE**, you're* being is exalted, never letting go of the **LOVE** that possesses your heart and keeps you pure from insecurities.

Sing forth with a voice of determination and let flow all words of knowledge.

We cannot disregard all those negative feelings amongst the people without understanding the ramifications.

LOVE is what we need to live; it is the lifeblood of our souls.

Keep free the flow of **LOVE** to and from the heart, and **GOD** will bless our lives.

For his one commandment of **LOVE** thyself, so you can **LOVE** your neighbor,

It is to be practiced within the context of giving without expecting a reward.

It is better to reward yourself with the knowledge of knowing that you have given **LOVE** to others and yourself.

APPENDIX

Healing through Writing Steps

1. Obtain paper and pen or pencil or sit at the computer keyboard and type it out.
2. Take three deep breaths and exhale as oxygen relaxes the body. Then ask **GOD** to place a white light of **LOVE** around your being. The reason for this is that when writing down the issues, emotions will be raw and the white light of **LOVE** will help keep the mind on completing the exercise.
3. Next write down or type out the issue(s) in as much detail as you feel your need to.
4. After each one, say it out loud and then say this PRAYER: *"My dear GOD, I am giving this (name of problem or fear) to you. I do not need it. I am releasing it from my mind, heart and soul. It is no longer serving me to my highest and best good. I ask that you fill my being with your LOVE, forgiveness and understanding. I thank you for this lesson and those who taught it to me and now I am moving on. I LOVE you my dear GOD. Amen".*
5. After completion of the writing session, take the paper and rip it up and throw it into the trash.
6. The next step is to sit down and take three deep breaths and exhale. Then image surrounding the body with a white light of **GOD's LOVE** and **PEACE**. Let the energy flow through the body and repeat the following: "*I am LOVED, I LOVE myself, I am worthy and deserving of LOVE and forgiveness of myself and my abuser(s)*." Repeat this affirmation as many times as needed. The more this is said, the more the mind begins to believe it.
7. Next is to ask ARCHANGEL Michael to cut any remaining karmatic relationship cords with your abuser(s). This is done as we sit in a chair and imagine yourself in a room with your abuser(s) sitting across from us with a cord coming from their heart to our heart. Place the abuser(s) in a white light of **LOVE** and ask ARCHANGEL Michael to enter the room and with his blue sword of light to cut the karmatic cords. Say this **PRAYER**: *"Dear ARCHANGEL Michael I ask you to cut all and any remaining karmatic cords with your LOVING blue sword. I am*

sorry that I have offended (say the name of the person sitting across from you) and I release all attachments that created the negative karma with us. I command they be gone now! Thank you ARCHANGEL Michael, I LOVE you".

8. See the cords fall to the ground and shrivel up into nothing. Tell your abuser(s) *"We are done, you are forgiven, thank you for the lessons, I LOVE you, you may leave now."* Image seeing them get up and leave the room through a door and the door shutting behind them. Then thank ARCHANGEL Michael and you leave the room through a door into a bright light of *LOVE*.

Cleaning Negative Energies with Sage

Please do not do this exercise if you are allergic to sage

1. To clean or clear that energy from our living space is done by using sage wands. These can be bought at any new age bookstore. (Please do not use and set fire to the sage seasoning that is use in the dressing we stuff the Thanksgiving turkey with. *It is not the same thing and not safe to burn*). When you light the wands, they will emit a fair amount of smoke.

2. Open a window to let out the energies that are being cleared. Clearing requires letting sage smoke into the entire living space, including closets and cabinets.

3. Waving the wand through cabinet space and closets is sufficient, and then shut the door afterwards.

4. For rooms, walk around once in a circle to allow the smoke to fill the area including the corners. It does not require filling the room with a dense fog of sage smoke to accomplish the goal.

5. As the sage smoke filters through each room, cabinet and closet, say *"If you are not of the light, you must leave. I bless this area with the LOVE and light of Jesus Christ. Amen"*.

6. When done, make sure to extinguish the sage and close the window. I usually dip the ends of the sage into a shallow level of water. Cleaning and blessing can be done on a regular basis as needed.

Channeling in our ANGELS Messages

1. Find a quiet area, and sit with paper, pen or pencil or type it out on the keyboard.
2. Take three deeps breaths for relaxation and to clear the mind.
3. Then say the following PRAYER: "*My dear ANGELS, I am LOVINGLY asking that you bring to me your words of wisdom that will help me grow SPIRITUALLY through my writing. I am ready now to receive your words of LOVE. Please tell me your name after each message and let me know when the session is over. Thank you my blessed ANGELS*".
4. When the messages come, they will be **SPIRITUAL** in nature and different from our ego based thoughts. The words may come fast, and if you cannot keep up ask your **ANGELS** kindly to slow down, please.
5. At the end of the writing session, thank your ANGELS for their insight and wisdom.

Reaffirmations of Love and Abundance

- I am **LOVE** and give **LOVE** to all I see.
- I am wealthy in all areas of my life and am full of **ABUNDANCE** and I thank the universe and **GOD** everyday for my wealth and **ABUNDANCE**.
- I **PRAY** for all my family and friends that they are filled everyday with **GOD's LOVE** and **ABUNDANCE**.
- I am worthy and deserving of all the riches the universe has to offer.
- I chose to visualize and attract money and love to flow to me freely just as I give money and love freely to others.
- I forgive all those who have hurt me in the past. I let go of the ego that keeps me from moving forward.
- I have no fear as I am letting go all of all negativity and ego.
- I am grateful to the good Lord for providing me with what I need and what I have.

Tube of Light Protection PRAYER

BELOVED I AM Presence bright,
Round me seal your Tube of Light
From Ascended Master flame

Called forth now in *GOD's* own name.
Let it keep my temple free
From all discord sent to me.
I AM calling forth Violet Fire
To blaze and transmute all desire,
Keeping on in Freedom's name
Till *I AM* one with the Violet Flame.

Recap of the PRAYERs in the book

1. My dear *GOD*, please *take away these negative blockages* that are hindering and stopping me from achieving a happy life of *LOVE*, belonging and success. I ask that you fill my heart, mind and soul with your *LOVE* instead. I thank you and *LOVE* you my dear *GOD*. Amen.

2. Dear *GOD* and my dear **ANGELS**. I ask you to *take away the negativity from my being*. I am releasing all the fear, anger, sadness, and mistrust to you. Please help me to let go of the need to control everything. I ask your help in *LOVING* others instead of criticism by filling my heart, mind and soul with *LOVE*. I thank you and I *LOVE* you my dear *GOD* and **ANGELS**. Amen.

3. My dear *GOD*, *fill me with LOVE for (name of family member)* and take this anger way now. Bring **PEACE** to my mind now. I *LOVE* you and thank you, Amen.

4. Dear Lord, I ask you to fill my heart with *LOVE* and understanding for those around me. *Help me to guide others, and to be strong against the need to control, dictate and judge others harshly*. Help me to know the difference between what I can take care of and what I cannot. I *LOVE* you and thank my dear Lord. Amen.

5. My dear Lord, *I give you my guilt* for I am worthy and deserving of what you are giving me through others. Let me thank you for your blessings bestowed upon me and grant me **HAPPINESS** in knowing you *LOVE* and care for me. Thank you and I *LOVE* you my dear Lord, Amen.

6. My dear Lord, help me now to *release these destructive feelings*. I do not need them. Let your *LOVE* fill my being and give me understanding and patience in this situation. Thank you my dear Lord, I *LOVE* you. Amen.

7. My dear *GOD*, I am *giving this (name of problem or fear) to you now*. I do not need it. I am releasing it from my mind, heart and soul. It is no longer serving me to my

highest and best good. I ask that you fill my being with your *LOVE*, forgiveness and understanding. I thank you for this lesson and those who taught it to me and now I am moving on. I *LOVE* you my dear *GOD*. Amen.

8. I am *LOVED*, I *LOVE* myself, I am worthy and deserving of *LOVE* and forgiveness of myself and my abuser(s).

9. Dear *GOD*, the universe and my dear *ANGELS*, _please take away this bad memory_ from me now. I do not need the memory; I am giving it to you now. Please fill my mind with your *LOVE* and *PEACE*. I *LOVE* and forgive myself, and thank you for taking the bad memory away. Amen.

10. Dear ARCHANGEL Michael I ask you to _cut these bad and negative memories_ with your blue light of *LOVE* to release these memories. I am sorry to those I have offended that created the negative memories and I command they be gone now! Thank you ARCHANGEL Michael, I *LOVE* you.

11. My dear *ANGELS*, I am *LOVINGLY* asking that you bring to me your words of wisdom that will _help me grow SPIRITUALLY through my writing_. I am ready now to receive your words of *LOVE*. Please tell me your name after each message and let me know when the session is over. Thank you my blessed *ANGELS*.

12. My dear *GOD* and my *ANGELS* I give you my fears, and my insecurities. _I am releasing_ all of them from my soul, mind and body into your hands. I ask that you fill me with your *LOVE*, assurance, *ABUNDANCE*, and blessings. I ask for your guidance and to show me what I need to do. I ask this of you. I thank you and I *LOVE* you.

13. Dear *GOD*, my *ANGELS* and universe. I ask that you _take away from me this desperation_ that is causing me the grief, pain and sorrow I am experiencing. I ask that you fill my heart; mind and soul with your *LOVE* of understanding and grace. Please lead me to those resources and people who can help me overcome this. I need your help this moment. I ask that you help me remove myself from the situation(s) in order for me to heal. I ask this of you my dear Lord *GOD*. Thank you and I *LOVE* you. Amen.

14. My dear *GOD*, I asked you to _take this memory away now_. I do not need it. I *LOVE* you and thank you. Amen.

15. Dear *GOD*, be with me now and _take this fear away_ from my mind and presence. I give it to you. Please fill me with

your **LOVE** and **PEACE** to calm my fears. I **LOVE** you, I **LOVE** myself, and the fear is now gone. Thank you and Amen.

16. Dear **GOD**, please give me the strength to _overcome this anxiety_. Do not let me burden my family and friends with this anxiety. Please take it away now. I **LOVE** you and thank you.

17. My dear **GOD**, I am asking you **LOVINGLY** to _please take this anger and hurt from my being now_. I am giving it to you to keep. I am free of this emotional baggage that has caused me to not **LOVE** myself and others in a healthy way. I ask that you fill my mind, soul and body with your everlasting **LOVE** now. Thank you my dear **GOD**, I **LOVE** you and Amen.

18. Dear **GOD**, my **ANGELS** and guides, _I ask of you to help me find my BELOVED_ who is meant for me. I also ask that you help me to release any doubts, fears, anxieties, neediness and desperation that will keep me from trusting your guidance. I also ask that you fill my heart with self **LOVE** and help me to forgive all those who have not **LOVED** me, and who have hurt me throughout my life. And I am sorry to all those who I have hurt and caused pain. I ask this my dear Lord with **LOVE** and thanks. Amen.

19. Dear Lord, help me now to _overcome this (negative feeling)_. Please take it away, I do not want it. I am replacing this (negative feeling) with your **LOVE**. I **LOVE** and thank you. Amen.

Web sites

Chakra information:
http://www.expressionsofSPIRIT.com/yoga/chakras.htm

Doreen Virtues website on ANGEL therapy:
http://www.ANGELtherapy.com/about_at.php.

Hawaiian healing system: http://www.self-i-dentity-through-hooponopono.com/contact.htm

Musically toned crystal healing bowls:
http://www.saggiohealingarts.com/crystalsingingbowls.html

www.purpleplates.com 1-860-830-9069.

Vision Quest Bookstore, Scottsdale Arizona. This bookstore offers phone readings. I have been using them for years and the psychics are not shams.
http://www.visionquestbooks.com/

Made in the USA
Charleston, SC
24 December 2012